"One of the masterpieces of St. Alphonsus, a book that speaks to all hearts...a very highly-prized and best-selling work."

THE PRACTICE OF THE LOVE OF JESUS CHRIST

(A Commentary on 1 *Cor.* 13:4-7, *"Love is patient, love is kind..."*)

BY

SAINT ALPHONSUS LIGUORI
(1696-1787)
DOCTOR OF THE CHURCH
Bishop of Saint Agatha, and Founder of the
Congregation of the Most Holy Redeemer

Taken from Volume VI of
THE ASCETICAL WORKS
OF ST. ALPHONSUS,
THE HOLY EUCHARIST

TRANSLATED FROM THE ITALIAN
EDITED BY
REV. EUGENE GRIMM, C.Ss.R.
NEW YORK, CINCINNATI, AND ST. LOUIS:
1887

Edited and language modernized by Darrell Wright,
2016

CONTENTS: (Page numbers in as in *The Holy Eucharist, in* [ ])

The Practice of the Love of Jesus Christ

WE have here one of the masterpieces of St. Alphonsus, a book that speaks to all hearts, that reveals to
every Christian soul its true needs and the true means
to satisfy them. One cannot read this book without becoming better; nor can one grow tired in reading it
again and again. It is indeed a very highly-prized and
widely-spread work. It was published in 1768.

The holy bishop, developing the celebrated text of St.
Paul on the qualities of true love, explains in thirteen
chapters the principal virtues that we ought to practice
and the defects that we ought to avoid in order to render
to our Lord love for love. He treats of patience in general (Chap. 1), and in particular in sicknesses, poverty,
and contempt (Chap. 10); of meekness (Chaps. 2 and
8); of purity of intention (Chap. 3); of tepidity, and the
remedies against this vice, namely, the desire of perfection, the determination to attain perfection, mental prayer,
frequent communion, and prayer (Chap. 4); of humility
(Chap. 5); of ambition and vain-glory (Chap. 6); of detachment from all things, especially when there is question
of following one's vocation (Chap. 7); of conformity to
the will of God, and of obedience (Chap. 9); of faith
(Chap. 11); of hope (Chap. 12); and, finally, of temptations, and spiritual desolation (Chap. 13). The work is
concluded by a summary of virtues that are to be practiced. ED

Introduction

1.

How Deserving Jesus Christ is of our Love, on Account of the Love He has Shown Us in His Passion

THE whole sanctity and perfection of a soul consists in loving Jesus Christ, our God, our sovereign good, and our Redeemer. Whoever loves me, says Jesus Christ himself, shall be loved by my Eternal Father: *My Father loves you because you have loved Me.*1 Some, says St. Francis de Sales,2 make perfection consist in an austere life; others in prayer; others in frequenting the Sacraments; others in alms-deeds. But they deceive themselves: perfection consists in loving God with our whole heart. The Apostle wrote : *Above all things, . . . have love, which is the bond of perfection.*3 It is love which keeps united and preserves all the virtues that render a man perfect. Hence St. Augustine said: "Love God, and do whatever you please;"4 because a soul that loves God is taught by that same love never to do anything that will displease him, and to leave nothing undone that may please him.

But perhaps God does not deserve all our love? *He has loved us with an everlasting love.*5 O man, says the Lord, behold I was the first to love you. You were

1 "Ipse enim Pater amat vos, quia vos me amastis." John 16.27.
2 *Spirit of St Francis de Sales*, Part 1, ch. 25.
3 "Super omnia, . . . charitatem habete, quod est vinculum perfectionis."
Col. 3.14.
4 "Ama, et fac quod vis."
5 "In charitate perpetua dilexi te." Jer. 31.3.

[264] not yet in the world, even the world itself was not, and I already loved you. As long as I am God, I loved you; as long as I have loved myself, I have also loved you. With good reason, therefore, did St. Agnes, that young holy virgin, reply to those who wished to unite her to an earthly spouse: "I am engaged to another lover."1 "Go," said she, "O lovers of this world, cease to pursue my love; my God was the first to love me. He has loved me from all eternity: it is but just, then, for me to give him all my affections, and to love none other but him."

As Almighty God knew that man is won by kindness, he determined to lavish his gifts upon him, and so take captive the affections of his heart. For this reason he said, *I will draw them with the cords of Adam, with the bands of love.*2 I will catch men by those very snares by which they are naturally caught, that is, by the snares of love. And such exactly are all the favors of God to man. After having given him a soul created in his own image, with memory, understanding, and will, and a body with its senses, he created heaven and earth for him, yes, all that exists, all for the love of man: the firmament, the stars, the planets, the seas, the rivers, the fountains, the hills, the plains, metals, fruits, and a countless variety of animals: and all these creatures that they might minister to the uses of man, and that man might love Him in gratitude for so many admirable gifts.

"Heaven and earth, and all things, tell me to love You,"3 says St. Augustine. "My Lord," he said, "whatever I behold on the earth, or above the earth, all speak to me, and exhort me to love You; because all assure me that You have made them for the love of me."

1 "Ab alio amatore praeventa sum."
2 "In funiculis Adam traham eos, in vinculis charitatis." Hosea 11.4.
3 "Coelum et terra et omnia mihi dicunt, ut te amem." *Confessions*, Bk. 10, ch. 6.

[265] The Abbot de Ranee, founder of La Trappe, when from his hermitage he stood and surveyed the hills, the fountains, the birds, the flowers, the planets, and the skies, felt himself animated by each one of these creatures to love that God who had created all through love to him.

In like manner St. Mary Magdalene de Pazzi, when she held any beautiful flower in her hand, was enkindled by the sight of it with love to God; and she would say: "And God, then, has thought from all eternity of creating this flower for love of me!" Thus did that flower become, as it were, a dart of love, which sweetly wounded her, and united her more and more to her God.

On the other hand, St. Teresa, at the sight of trees, fountains, rivers, lakes, or meadows, declared that all these fair things upbraided her for her ingratitude in loving so coldly a God who created them that he might be loved by her.

But God was not satisfied with giving us so many beautiful creatures. He has gone to such lengths to gain our love, as to give himself to us. The Eternal Father did not hesitate to give us even his only-begotten Son: *For God so loved the world as to give His only-begotten Son.*1

1 "Sic enim Deus dilexit mundum, ut Filium unigenitum daret."

John 3.16.

[266] When the Eternal Father saw that we were all dead, and deprived of his grace by sin, what did he do? for the immense love, even, as the Apostle writes, for the too great love he bore us, he sent his beloved Son to make atonement for us; and so to restore to us that life which sin had robbed us of: *Who through his exceeding love with which He loved us, even when we were dead in sins, has brought us to life together in Christ.*1 And in granting us his Son (not sparing his Son, that he might spare us), he has granted us every good together with him, his grace, his love, and paradise, since assuredly all these gifts are much less than that of his Son: *He that spared not even His own Son, but delivered Him up for us all, how has He not also with Him given us all things?*2

And so, likewise, the Son, through his love towards us, has given himself wholly to us: *Who loved me, and delivered Himself for me.*3 In order to redeem us from everlasting death, and to recover for us the divine grace and heaven which we had forfeited, he became man, and put on flesh like our own: *And the Word was made flesh.*4 Behold, then, a God reduced to nothingness: *But emptied Himself, taking the form of a servant, . . . and in the likeness of man.*5 Behold the sovereign of the world humbling himself so low as to assume the form of a servant, and to subject himself to all the miseries which the rest of men endure.

But what is more astonishing still is, that he could very well have saved us without dying and without suf-

1 "Propter nimiam charitatem suam qua dilexit nos, et cum essemus mortui peccatis, convivificavit nos in Christo." Eph. 2.4.

2 "Qui etiam proprio Filio suo non pepercit, sed pro nobis omnibus tradidit illum: quomodo non etiam cum illo omnia nobis donavit?" Rom. 8.32.
3 "Dilexit me, et tradidit semetipsum pro me." Gal. 2.20.
4 "Et Verbum caro factum est." John 1.14.
5 "Exinanivit semetipsum formam servi accipiens, . . . et habitu inventus ut homo." Phil. 2.7.

[267] faring at all; but no: he chose a life of sorrow and contempt, and a death of bitterness and ignominy even to the expiring on a cross, the gibbet of infamy, the award of vilest criminals: *He humbled Himself, becoming obedient unto death, even to the death of the cross.*1 But why, if he could have ransomed us without suffering, why should he choose to die, and to die on a cross? To show us how he loved us. *He loved us, and delivered Himself for us.*2 He loved us, and because he loved us, he delivered himself up to sorrows, and disgraces, and to a death more cruel than ever any man endured in this world.

Hence that great lover of Jesus Christ, St. Paul, took occasion to say: *The love of Christ presses us.*3 Wishing to show us by these words that it is not so much the sufferings themselves of Jesus Christ as his love in enduring them, that obliges us, and, as it were, constrains us to love him. Let us hear what St. Francis de Sales says on this text: "When we remember that Jesus Christ, true God, has loved us to such an excess as to suffer death, and the death of the cross, for us, our hearts are, as it were, put in a wine-press, and suffer violence, until love be extorted from them, but a violence which, the stronger it is, becomes the more delightful."4 He then goes on to say, "Ah! why do we not therefore cast ourselves on Jesus crucified, to die on the cross with him, who has chosen to die for love of us? I will hold him (should we say), and I will never let him go; I will die

with him, and will be consumed in the flames of his love.
One flame shall consume this divine Creator and his
miserable creature. My Jesus gives himself unreservedly
to me, and I give myself unreservedly to him. I will live

1 "Humiliavit semetipsum, factus obediens usque ad mortem,
mortem autem crucis." Phil. 2.8.
2 "Dilexit nos, et tradidit semetipsum pro nobis." Eph. 5.2.
3 "Charitas Christi urget nos." 2 Cor. 5.14.
4 *On the Love of God*, Bk. 7, ch. 8.

[268] and die on his loving breast; neither life nor death
shall ever separate me from him. O eternal love, my soul
longs after You, and makes choice of You forever.
Come, O Holy Spirit, and inflame our hearts with love.
O love, O death, to die to all other loves, to live solely to
that of Jesus Christ! O Redeemer of our souls, grant
that we may eternally sing, Live, Jesus! I love Jesus;
live, Jesus, whom I love! yes, I love Jesus, who reigns
for evermore."1

The love of Jesus Christ towards men created in him
a longing desire for the moment of his death, when his
love should be fully manifested to them; hence he was
wont to say in his lifetime: *I have a baptism with which I
am to be baptized, and how am I constrained until it be
accomplished!*2 I have to be baptized in my own blood;
and how do I feel myself straitened with the desire that the
hour of my Passion may soon arrive; for then man will
know the love which I bear him! Hence St. John, speaking of that night in which Jesus began his Passion, writes:
*Jesus knowing that His hour was come, that He should
pass out of this world to the Father, having loved His
own who were in the world, He loved them unto the end.*3
The Redeemer called that hour His own hour, because the

time of his death was the time desired by him; as it was then that he wished to give mankind the last proof of his love, by dying for them upon a cross overwhelmed by sorrows.

But what could have ever induced a God to die as a malefactor upon a cross between two sinners, with such insult to his divine majesty? "Who did this?" asks St.

1 *On the Love of God,* Bk. 12, ch. 13.
2 "Baptismo habeo baptizari; et quomodo coarctor usquedum perficiatur!" Luke 12.50.
3 "Sciens Jesus quia venit hora ejus, ut transeat ex hoc mundo ad Patrem, cum dilexisset suos, ... in finem dilexit eos." John 13.1.

[269] Bernard; he answers, "It was love, careless of its dignity."1 Ah, love indeed, when it tries to make itself known, does not seek what is becoming to the dignity of the lover, but what will serve best to declare itself to the object loved. St. Francis of Paula therefore had good reason to cry out at the sight of a crucifix, "O love, O love, O love!" And in like manner, when we look upon Jesus on the cross, we should all exclaim, O love, O love, O love!

Ah, if faith had not assured us of it, who could ever have believed that a God, almighty, most happy, and the Lord of all, should have condescended to love man to such an extent that he seems to go out of himself for the love of him? We have seen Wisdom itself, that is the Eternal Word, become foolish through the excessive love he bore to man! So spoke St. Laurence Justinian: "We see Wisdom itself infatuated through excess of love."2 St. Mary Magdalene de Pazzi said the same: One day, being in ecstasy, she took a wooden crucifix in her hands, and then cried out: "Yes, my Jesus, You are mad with love: I repeat it, and I will say it forever: My Jesus, You are mad with love." But no, says St. Denis the Areopagite; "no, it is not madness, but the ordinary effect of divine love, which makes him who loves go out of himself, in order to give himself up entirely to the object of his love: divine love causes ecstasy."3

Oh, if men would only pause and consider, looking at Jesus on the cross, the love that he has borne each one of them! "With what love," says St. Francis de Sales, "would not our souls become enkindled at the sight of those flames which are in the Redeemer s breast! And oh, what happiness, to be able to be consumed by that

1 "Quis hoc fecit? Fecit amor, dignitatis nescius." *On the Song of Songs*, sermon 61.
2 Vidimus Sapientiam amoris nimietate infatuatam." *Sermon on the Nature of God*
3 "Extasim facit divinus amor." *On the Names of God*, ch. 4.

[270] same fire with which our God burns for us! What joy, to be united to God by the chains of love!" St. Bona-venture called the wounds of Jesus Christ, wounds which pierce the most senseless hearts, and which inflame the most icy souls.1 How many darts of love come forth from those wounds, to wound the hardest hearts! Oh, what flames issue from the burning heart of Jesus Christ to inflame the coldest souls! And chains, how many, from that wounded side, to bind the most stubborn wills!

The Venerable John of Avila, who was so possessed with the love of Jesus Christ that he never failed in any of his sermons to speak of the love which Jesus Christ bears towards us, in a treatise on the love which this most loving Redeemer has for men, has expressed himself in sentiments so full of the fire of devotion, and of such beauty, that I desire to insert them here. He says as follows:

"You, O Redeemer, have loved man in such a manner, that whoso reflects upon this love cannot do less than love You; for Thy love offers violence to hearts: as the Apostle says : *The love of Christ presses us.*2 The source of the love of Jesus Christ for men is his love for God. Hence he said on Holy Thursday, *That the world may know that I love the Father, arise, let us from here.*3 But to where? To die for men upon the cross." "No human intellect can conceive how strongly this fire burns in the heart of Jesus Christ. As he was commanded to suffer death once, so, had he been commanded to die a thousand times, his love had been sufficient to endure it. And if what he suffered for all men had been

1 "Vulnera, corda saxea vulnerantia, et mentes congelatas inflammantia."
Stim. div. am. Pt. 1, ch. 1.
2 "Charitas Christi urget nos." 2 Cor. 5.14.
3 "Ut cognoscat mundus quia diligo Patrem, . . . surgite, eamus." John 14.31.

[271] imposed upon him for the salvation of one single soul, he would have done the same for each in particular as he did for all. And as he remained three hours upon the cross, so, had it been necessary, his love would have made him remain there even to the day of judgment. So that Jesus Christ loved much more than he suffered. O divine love, how far greater were you than you outwardly seem to be; for though so many wounds

and bruises tell us of great love, still they do not tell
all its greatness. There was far more within than that
which appeared externally. That was but as a spark
which bounded forth from the vast ocean of infinite love.
This is the greatest mark of love, to lay down our life for
our friends. But this was not a sufficient mark for Jesus
Christ with which to express his love."

"This is the love which causes holy souls to lose themselves, and to stand amazed, when once they have been
allowed to know it. From it spring those burning sentiments of ardor, the desire of martyrdom, joy in sufferings, exultation under the storms of distress, the force to
walk on burning coals as if they were roses, a thirst for
sufferings, rejoicing in that which the world dreads, embracing that which it abhors. St. Ambrose says that the
soul which is espoused to Jesus Christ upon the cross,
thinks nothing so glorious as to bear upon itself the
marks of the crucified one."

"But how, O my lover, shall I repay this your love!
It is right that blood should be compensated by blood.
May I behold myself dyed in this blood and nailed to
this cross! O holy cross, receive me also! O crown of
thorns, enlarge yourself, that I too may place you on my
head! O nails, leave those innocent hands of my Lord,
and come and pierce my heart with compassion and with
love! For You, my Jesus, didst die, as St. Paul says,
in order to gain dominion over the living and the dead,
not by means of chastisements, but by love:" *For to this*
[272] *end Christ died and rose again: that He might be
Lord both of the dead and of the living.*1

"O robber of hearts, the strength of Your love has
broken the exceeding hardness of our hearts! You have

inflamed the whole world with Your love. O most loving Lord, inebriate our hearts with this wine, consume them with this fire, pierce them with this dart of Your love! Your Cross is indeed an arrow which pierces hearts. May all the world know that my heart is smitten! O sweetest love, what have You done? You have come to heal me, and You have wounded me. You have come to teach me, and You have made me nearly mad. O madness full of wisdom, may I never live without you! All, O Lord, that I behold upon the cross invites me to love You : the wood, the figure, the wounds of Your body; and above all, Your love, engages me to love You, and never to forget You more."2
But in order to arrive at the perfect love of Jesus Christ, we must adopt the means. Behold, then, the means which St. Thomas Aquinas gives us:3

1. To have a constant remembrance of the benefits of God, both general and particular.

2. To consider the infinite goodness of God, who is ever waiting to do us good, and who ever loves us, and seeks from us our love.

3. To avoid even the smallest thing that could offend him.

4. To renounce all the sensible goods of this world, riches, honors, and sensual pleasures.

Father Tauler 4 says that meditation on the sacred Passion of Jesus Christ is a great means also for acquiring his perfect
love.

1 "In hoc enim Christus mortuus est et resurrexit, ut et mortuorum

et vivorum dominetur." Rom. 14.9.
2 *Disch. on the Love of God.*
3 *On the Two Precepts,* ch. 4.
4 Letter. 20.

[273] Who can deny that, of all devotions, devotion to
the Passion of Jesus Christ is the most useful, the most
tender, the most agreeable to God, one that gives the
greatest consolation to sinners, and at the same time
most powerfully enkindles loving souls? Whence is it
that we receive so many blessings, if it be not from the
Passion of Jesus Christ? Whence have we hope of
pardon, courage against temptations, confidence that we
shall go to heaven? Whence are so many lights to know
the truth, so many loving calls, so many spurrings to
change our life, so many desires to give ourselves up to
God, except from the Passion of Jesus Christ? The
Apostle therefore had but too great reason to declare
him to be excommunicated who did not love Jesus Christ.
*If any man love not our Lord Jesus Christ, let him be
anathema.*1

St. Bonaventure says there is no devotion more fitted
for sanctifying a soul than meditation on the Passion of
Jesus Christ; whence he advises us to meditate every
day upon the Passion, if we would advance in the love
of God. "If you would make progress, meditate daily
on the Passion of the Lord; for nothing works such an
entire sanctification in the soul, as the meditation of the
Passion of Christ."2 And before him St. Augustine, as
Bustis relates, said, that one tear shed in memory of the
Passion is worth more than to fast weekly on bread and
water fora year.3 Wherefore the saints were always oc-
cupied in considering the sorrows of Jesus Christ: it was
by this means that St. Francis of Assisi became a seraph.

1 "Si quis non amat Dominum nostrum Jesum Christum, sit
anathema." 1 Cor. 16.22.
2 "Si vis proficere, quotidie mediteris Domini passionem; nihil enim
in anima ita operatur universalem sanctimoniam, sicut meditatio
passionis Christi."
3 "Magis meretur vel unam lacrymam emittens ob memoriam
passionis Christi, quam si qualibet anni hebdomada in pane et aqua
jejunaret." *Rosar.*, Pt. 2, sermon 15.

[274] He was one day found by a gentleman shedding tears,
and crying out with a loud voice: being asked the cause
"I weep," he answered, "over the sorrows and disgraces
of my Lord: and what causes me the greatest sorrow
is, that men, for whom he suffered so much, live in forgetfulness of him." And on saying this he wept the
more, so that this gentleman began also himself to weep.
When the saint heard the bleating of a lamb, or saw
anything which reminded him of the Passion of Jesus,
he immediately shed tears. On another occasion, being
sick, some one told him to read some pious book. "My
book," he replied, "is Jesus crucified." Hence he did
nothing but exhort his brethren to be ever thinking of
the Passion of Jesus Christ. Tiepoli writes : "He who
becomes not inflamed with the love of God by looking
on Jesus dead upon the cross, will never love at all."

Affections and Prayers

O Eternal Word! You have spent three-and-thirty years in
labors and fatigues; You have given Your life and Your
blood for man s salvation; in short, You have spared nothing
to make men love You; and how is it possible that there
should be those who know this, and yet do not love You? O
God, amongst these ungrateful ones I also may be
numbered! I see the wrong I have done You; O my Jesus,
have pity upon me!

I offer You this ungrateful heart ungrateful it is true, but penitent. Yes, I repent above every other evil, O my dear Redeemer, for having despised You! I repent, and I am sorry with my whole heart. O my soul, love a God who is bound like a criminal for you; a God scourged like a slave for you; a God made a mock-king for you; a God, in short, dead upon a cross, as the vilest outcast for you! Yes, my Savior, my God, I love You, I love You! Bring continually to my remembrance, I beseech You, all that You have suffered for me, so that I may never more forget to love You. O cords that bound my Jesus, bind me to Jesus; thorns that crowned my Jesus, pierce me with the love of Jesus; nails that transfixed my Jesus, nail me to the Cross of Jesus, that I may live and die united to Jesus. O blood [275] of Jesus, inebriate me with his holy love! O death of Jesus, make me die to every earthly affection! Pierced feet of my Lord, I embrace you; deliver me from hell, which I have deserved; my Jesus, in hell I could no more love You, and yet I desire to love You always. Save me, my dearest Savior; bind me to Yourself, that I may never again lose You.

O Mary, refuge of sinners, and Mother of my Savior! help a sinner who wishes to love God, and who recommends himself to you; help me for the love you bear for Jesus Christ.

2.

How much Jesus Christ deserves to be Loved by us, on Account of the Love He has shown us in Instituting the most Holy Sacrament of the Altar

*Jesus, knowing that His hour was come, that He should pass out of this world to the Father: having loved His own . . . He loved them unto the end.*1 Our most loving Savior, knowing that his hour was now come for leaving this earth, desired, before he went to die for us, to leave us the greatest possible mark of his love; and this was the gift of the most Holy Sacrament.

St. Bernardine of Siena remarks, that men remember more continually and love more tenderly the signs of love which are shown to them in the hour of death.2 Hence it is the custom that friends, when about to die, leave to those persons whom they have loved some gift, such as a garment or a ring, as a memorial of their affection. But what have You, O my Jesus, left us, when quitting this world, in memory of Your love? Not, in deed, a garment or a ring, but Your own body, Your blood, Your soul, Your divinity, Your whole self, without

1 "Sciens Jesus quia venit hora ejus, ut transeat ex hoc mundo ad Patrem, cum dilexisset suos qui erant in mundo, in finem dilexit eos." John 13. 1.
2 "Quae in fine in signum amicitiae celebrantur, firmius memoriae imprimuntur, et cariora tenentur." Vol. 2. s. 54, a. 1, ch. 1.

[276] reserve. "He gave you all," says St. John Chrysostom; "He left nothing for himself."1

The Council of Trent says,2 that in this gift of the Eucharist Jesus Christ desired, as it were, to pour forth all the riches of the love he had for men. And the Apostle observes, that Jesus desired to bestow this gift upon men on the very night itself when they were planning his death: The same night in which He was betrayed, He took bread; and giving thanks, broke and said: *Take and eat: this is My body.*3 St. Bernardine of Siena says, that Jesus Christ, burning with love for us, and not content with being prepared to give his life for us, was constrained by the excess of his love to work a greater work before he died; and this was to give his own body for our food.4

This Sacrament, therefore, was rightly named by St. Thomas, "*the* Sacrament of love, the pledge of love."5 Sacrament of love; for love was the only motive which induced Jesus Christ to give us in it his whole self, Pledge of love; so that if we had ever doubted his love, we should have in this sacrament a pledge of it: as if our Redeemer, in leaving us this gift, had said: O souls, if you ever doubt my love, behold, I leave you myself in this Sacrament: with such a pledge, you can never any more doubt that I love you, and love you to excess. But more, St. Bernard calls this sacrament "the love of loves;"6 because this gift comprehends all the other gifts

1 "Totum tibi dedit, nihil sibi reliquit."
2 "Divitias divini sui erga homines amoris velut effudit." Sess. 13. ch. 2.
3 "In qua nocte tradebatur, accepit panem, et gratias agens fregit, et dixit: Accipite et manducate; hoc est corpus meum." 1 Cor. 11. 23.
4 "In illo fervoris excessu, quando paratus erat pro nobis mori, ab excessu amoris majus opus agere coactus est, quam umquam operatus fuit, dare nobis corpus in cibum." *Loc. cit.*
5 "Sacramentum charitatis, Pignus charitatis."
6 "Amor amorum."

[277] bestowed upon us by our Lord, creation, redemption, predestination to glory; so that the Eucharist is not only a pi-edge of the love of Jesus Christ, but of paradise, which he desires also to give us. "In which," says the Church, "a pledge of future glory is given us." 1 Hence St. Philip Neri could find no other name for Jesus Christ in the Sacrament save that of "love;" and so, when the holy Viaticum was brought to him, he was heard to exclaim, "Behold my love; give me my love."

The prophet Isaiah 2 desired that the whole world should know the tender inventions that our God has made use of, with which to make men love him. And who could ever have thought if he himself had not done it that the Incarnate Word would hide himself under the appearances of bread, in order to become himself our food? "Does it not seem folly," says St. Augustine, "to say, *Eat my flesh; drink my blood*?"3 When Jesus Christ revealed to his disciples the sacrament he desired to leave them, they could not bring themselves to believe him; and they left him, saying: *How can this Man give us His flesh to eat? . . . This saying is hard, and who can hear it?*4 But that which men could neither conceive nor believe, the great love of Jesus Christ has thought of and accomplished. Take ye, and eat, said he to his disciples before he went to die; and through them to us all. Receive and eat: but what food shall that be, O Savior of the world, which You desire to give us before You die? *Take and eat; this is my body.*5

1 "In quo . . . futurae gloriae nobis pignus datur."
2 Isa. 12.4.
3 "Nonne videtur insania: Manducate meam carnem, bibite meum sanguinem?" *In Ps.* 33. en. 1.
4 "Quomodo potest hic nobis carnem suam dare ad manducandum? Durus est hic sermo; et quis potest eum audire?" John 6.53,61.
5 "Accipite et manducate; hoc est corpus meum."

[278] This is not earthly food; it is I myself who give myself entirely to you.

And oh, with what desire does Jesus Christ want to come into our souls in the Holy Communion! *With desire I have desired to eat this passover with you before I suffer.*1 So he spoke on that night in which he instituted this sacrament of love. With desire I have desired: so did the excessive love which he bore us cause him to speak, as St. Laurence Justinian remarks: "These are the words of most burning love."2 And in order that everyone might easily receive him, he desired to leave himself under the appearance of bread; for if he had left himself under the appearance of some rare or very costly food, the poor would have been deprived of him; but no, Jesus would hide himself under the form of bread, which costs but little, and can be found everywhere, in order that all in every country might be able to find him and receive him.

In order, then, to excite us to receive him in the Holy Communion, he not only exhorts us to do so by so many invitations, *Come, eat My bread; and drink the wine which I have mingled for you;*3 *Eat, O friends, and drink,*4 speaking of this heavenly bread and wine, but he even gives us a formal precept: *Take, and eat; this is My body.* And more than this; that we may go and receive him, he entices us with the promise of paradise. *He that eats My flesh has everlasting life. He that eats this bread shall live forever.*5 And still more, he threatens us with hell, and exclusion from paradise, if we refuse to communicate. *Except you eat the flesh of the Son of Man, you shall not*

1 "Desiderio desideravi hoc pascha manducare vobiscum." Luke 22.15.
2 "Flagrantissimae charitatis est vox haech." *De Tr. Chr. Ag.* ch. 2.
3 "Venite, comedite panem meum, et bibite vinum quod miscui vobis." Prov. 9.5.
4 "Comedite, amici, et bibite." Song of Songs, 5.1.
5 "Qui manducat meam carnem, . . . habet vitam aeternam. Qui manducat hunc panem, vivet in aeternum." John 6.55, 59.

[279] *have life in you.*1 These invitations, these promises, these threats, all proceed from the great desire he has to come to us in this sacrament.

But why is it that Jesus Christ so desires that we
should receive him in the Holy Communion? Here is
the reason. St. Denis says that love always sighs after
and tends to union, and so also says St. Thomas,
"Lovers desire of two to become one."2 Friends who
really love each other would like to be so united as to
become one person. Now this is what the infinite love
of God for man has done; that he would not only give
us himself in the eternal kingdom, but even in this life
would permit men to possess him in the most intimate
union, by giving them himself, whole and entire, under
the appearances of bread in the sacrament. He stands
there as though behind a wall; and from thence he be
holds, as it were, through a closed lattice: *Behold He stands
behind our wall, looking through the windows, looking
through the lattices.*3 It is true, we do not see him; but
he sees us, and is there really present: he is present, in
order that we may possess him: but he hides himself
from us to make us desire him: and as long as we have
not reached our true country, Jesus desires to give himself wholly to us, and to remain united with us.

He could not satisfy his love by giving himself to the
human race by his Incarnation and by his Passion, dying
for all men upon the cross; but he desired to find out
a way whereby he might give himself entirely to each
one of us in particular; and for this end he instituted
the Sacrament of the Altar, in order to unite himself
wholly to each: *He that eats My flesh, he said, abides in*

1 "Nisi manducaveritis carnem Filii hominis, . . . non habebitis
vitam in vobis." John 6.54.
2 "Amantes desiderant ex ambobus fieri unum." *S. Theol.* 1-2, q. 28,
a. 1.

3 "En ipse stat post parietem nostrum respiciens per fenestras, prospiciens per cancellos." Song of Songs, 2.9.

[280] *me and I in him.*1 In Holy Communion Jesus unites himself to the soul, and the soul to Jesus; and this is not a union of mere affection, but it is a true and real union. Hence St. Francis de Sales says: "In no other action can the Savior be considered more tender or more lov- ing than in this, in which he annihilates himself, so to say, and reduces himself to food, in order to penetrate our souls, and to unite himself to the hearts of his faith ful."2 St. John Chrysostom says that Jesus Christ, through the ardent love which he bore us, desired so to unite himself to us, as to become one and the same thing with us. "He mingled himself with us, that we might be one thing; for this is the property of those who ardently love."3

"It was Your wish, in short," says St. Laurence Justi- nian, "O God, enamoured of our souls, to make, by means of this sacrament, Your own heart, by an inseparable union, one and the same heart with ours!"4 St. Bernar- dine of Siena adds, that "the gift of Jesus Christ to us as our food was the last step of his love; since he gives himself to us in order to unite himself wholly to us; in the same way as food becomes united with him who par- takes of it."5 Oh, how delighted is Jesus Christ to be united with our souls! He one day said to his beloved servant, Margaret of Ypres, after Communion, "See, my daughter, the beautiful union that exists between me

1 "Qui manducat meam carnem, ... in me manet, et ego in illo." John 6.57.
2 *Introduction to the Devout Life,* Pt. 2, ch. 21.
3 "Semetipsum nobis immiscuit, ut unum quid simus; ardenter enim amantium hoc est." *Ad pop. Ant. hom.* 61.

4 "O quam mirabilis est dilectio tua, Domine Jesu, qui tuo corpori taliter nos incorporari voluisti, ut tecum unum cor et unam animam haberemus inseparabiliter colligatam!" *De Incarn. div. am.* ch. 5.
5 "Ultimus gradus amoris est, cum se dedit nobis in cibum; quia dedit se nobis ad omnimodam unionem, sicut cibus et cibans invicem uniuntur." Vol. 2, s. 54, a. 4, ch. 1.

[281] and you: come, then, love me; and let us remain ever united in love, and let us never separate again."

We must, then, be persuaded that a soul can neither do, nor think of doing, anything which gives greater pleasure to Jesus Christ than to communicate frequently, with dispositions suitable to the great guest whom she has to receive into her heart. I have said suitable, not indeed worthy dispositions; for if worthy were necessary, who could ever communicate? Another God would alone be worthy to receive God. By suitable, I mean such dispositions as become a miserable creature, clothed with the unhappy flesh of Adam. Ordinarily speaking, it is sufficient if a person communicates in a state of grace, and with a great desire of growing in the love of Jesus Christ. St. Francis de Sales said, "It is by love alone that we must receive Jesus Christ in the Communion, since it is through love alone that he gives himself to us."1 For the rest, with regard to the number of times a person should communicate, in this he should be guided by the advice of his spiritual Father. Nevertheless, we should be aware that no state of life or employment, neither the married state nor business, prevents frequent Communion, when the director thinks it advisable, as Pope Innocent XI has declared in his decree of 1679, when he says, "Frequent Communion must be left to the judgment of the confessors .... who, for lay persons in business, or in the marriage state, must recommend it according as they see it will be profitable for their salvation."2

We must next understand that there is nothing from
which we can derive such profit as from the Communion.
The Eternal Father has made Jesus Christ the possessor

1 *Introduction to the Devout Life,* Pt. 2, ch. 21.
2 "Frequens accessus (ad Eucharistiam) confessariorum judicio est
relinquendus, qui, . . . laicis negotiatoribus et conjugatis, quod
prospicient eorum saluti profuturum, id illis praescribere debebunt."

[282] of all his own heavenly treasures. *The Father has
given all things into His hands.*1 Hence, when Jesus Christ
comes to a soul in Holy Communion, he brings with
him boundless treasures of grace; and consequently
after Communion we can justly say, *Now all good things
came to me together with it.*2 St. Denis says that the Sacrament of the Eucharist is far more powerful for the
sanctification of souls than all other spiritual means of
grace;3 and St. Vincent Ferrer, that one Communion
does more for the soul than a week's fasting on bread
and water.

In the first place, as the Council of Trent teaches,
Communion is that great remedy which frees us from
venial, and preserves us against mortal sins.4 It is said
"from daily faults;" because according to St. Thomas,5
a man is excited by means of this sacrament to make
acts of love, by which venial sins are forgiven. And it
is said that "we are preserved from mortal sins, because
Communion increases grace, which will preserve us
from great faults. Hence Innocent III. says that Jesus
Christ delivered us from the power of sin by his Passion,
but that by the Eucharist he delivers us from the power
of sinning.6

This Sacrament, moreover, above all others, inflames our souls with divine love. *God is love.*7 And he is a fire which consumes all earthly affections in our hearts. *He is a consuming fire.*8 And for this very purpose,

1 "Omnia dedit ei Pater in manus." John 13.3.
2 "Venerunt mihi omnia bona pariter cum illa." Wisd. 7.11.
3 "Eucharistia maximam vim habet perficiendre sanctitatis."
4 "Antidotum quo liberemur a culpis quotidianis, et a peccatis mortalibus preservemur." Sess. 13. ch. 2.
5 *S. Theol.* Pt. 3, q. 79, a. 4.
6 "Per crucis mysterium, eripuit nos a potestate peccati; per Eucharistiae sacramentum, liberavit nos a voluntate peccandi." *De Alt. Myst.* Bk. 4, ch. 44.
7 "Deus charitas est." 1 John 4.8.
8 "Ignis consumens est." Deut. 4.24.

[283] namely, to enkindle this fire, the Son of God came upon earth. I am come to send fire on the earth; and He added, that he desired nothing but to see this fire enkindled in our souls: *And what will I but that it be kindled?*1 And oh, what flames of love does not Jesus Christ light up in the heart of every one who receives him devoutly in this sacrament! St. Catherine of Siena once saw the Host in a priest's hand appearing as a globe of fire; and the saint was astonished that the hearts of all men were not burned up, and, as it were, reduced to ashes by such a flame. Such brilliant rays issued from the face of St. Rose of Lima after Communion, as to dazzle the eyes of those who saw her; and the heat from her mouth was so intense, that a hand held near it was scorched. It is related of St. Wenceslaus, that by merely visiting the churches where the Blessed Sacrament was kept, he was inflamed by such an ardor, that his servant who accompanied him did not feel the cold, if when walking on the snow he trod in the footsteps of the saint.

St. John Chrysostom says that the most Holy Sacrament is a burning fire; so that when we leave the altar we breathe forth flames of love, which make us objects of terror to hell.2 The spouse of the Canticles says: *He brought me into the cellar of wine, He set in order love in me.* 3 St. Gregory of Nyssa says that Communion is precisely this cellar of wine, in which the soul becomes so inebriated with divine love, that it forgets and loses sight of creatures; and this is that languishing with love of which the spouse again speaks: *Stay me up with*

1 "Ignem veni mittere in terram; et quid volo, nisi ut accendatur?" Luke 12.49.
2 "Carbo cst Eucharistia, quae nos inflammat, ut tamquam leones ignem spirantes ab illa mensa recedamus, facti diabolo terribiles." *Ad pop. Ant. hom.* 61.
3 "Introduxit me in cellam vinariam, ordinavit in me charitatem." Song of Songs, 2.4.

[284] *flowers, compass me about with apples, because I languish with love.*1

Some one will say: "But this is the very reason why I do not communicate frequently, because I see that I am so cold in the love of God." Gerson answers such a one by saying : "Do you, therefore, because you are cold, willingly keep away from the fire? Rather, because you feel yourself cold, should you so much the more frequently approach this sacrament, if you really desire to love Jesus Christ." "Although it be with lukewarmness," wrote St. Bonaventure, "still approach, trusting in the mercy of God. The more one feels himself sick, the greater need has lie of a physician."2 In like manner, St, Francis de Sales: "Two sorts of persons ought to go frequently to Communion: the perfect, in order to remain so; and the imperfect, in order to be become per-

fect."3 But for frequent Communion, it is at least
necessary to have a great desire to become a saint and
to grow in the love of Jesus Christ. Our Lord said
once to St. Matilda: "When you go to Communion
desire all the love which a soul has ever had for me, and
I will receive your love according to your desire."4

Affections and Prayers

God of love, O infinite lover, worthy of infinite love, tell
me what more can You invent to make us love You? It
was not sufficient for You to become man, and to subject
Yourself to all our miseries; not sufficient to shed all Your blood
for us in torments, and then to die overwhelmed with sorrow,
upon a cross destined for the most shameful malefactors. You

1 "Fulcite me floribus, stipate me malis, quia amore langueo."
Song of Songs, 2.5.
2 "Licet tepide, tamen confidens de misericordia Dei accedat; tanto
magis aeger necesse habet requirere medicum, quanto magis senserit
se aegrotum." *De Prof. rel.* Bk. 2, ch. 77.
3 *Introduction to the Devout Life*, Pt. 2. ch. 21.
4 *Spir. Grat.* Bk. 3, ch. 22.

[285] did, at last, oblige Yourself to be hidden under the
species of bread and wine, to become our food, and so
united with each one of us. Tell me, I repeat, what more can
You invent to make Yourself loved by us? Ah, wretched
shall we be if we do not love You in this life! And when we
shall have entered into eternity, what remorse shall we not
feel for not having loved You! My Jesus, I will not die
without loving You, and loving You exceedingly! I am
heartily sorry, and am pained for having so greatly offended
You. But now I love You above all things. I love You more
than myself, and I consecrate to You all my affections. O
You, who inspire me with this desire, give me also grace to

accomplish it. My Jesus, my Jesus, I desire nothing of You but Yourself. Now that You have drawn me to Your love, I leave all, I renounce all, and I bind myself to You: You alone are sufficient for me.

Mary, Mother of God, pray to Jesus for me, and make me a saint! Add this also to the many wonders you have done in changing sinners into saints.

3.

The Great Confidence we ought to have in the Love which Jesus Christ has shown us and in all He has done for us.

David placed all his hope of salvation in his future Redeemer, and said: Into Your hands, O Lord, I commend my spirit; You have redeemed me, O Lord, the God of truth. But how much more ought we to place our confidence in Jesus Christ, now that he has come, and has accomplished the work of redemption! Hence each one of us should say, and repeat again and again with greater confidence: *Into Your hands, O Lord, I commend my spirit; You have redeemed me, O Lord, the God of truth.*1

If we have great reason to fear everlasting death on account of our sins against God, we have, on the other hand, far greater reason to hope for everlasting life through the merits of Jesus Christ, which are infinitely more powerful for our salvation than our sins are for

1 "In manus tuas commendo spiritum meum; redemisti me, Domine Deus veritatis." Ps. 30.6.

[286] our damnation. We have sinned, and have deserved

hell; but the Redeemer has come to take upon himself
all our offenses, and to make satisfaction for them by
His sufferings: *Surely He has borne our infirmities, and
carried our sorrows.*1

In the same unhappy moment in which we sinned, God
had already written against us the sentence of eternal
death; but what has our merciful Redeemer done? *Blot-
ting out the handwriting of the decree which was against us, . . . the same He took out of the way, fastening it
to the cross.*2 He canceled by his blood the decree of our
condemnation, and then fastened it to the cross, in order
that, when we look at the sentence of our damnation for
the sins we have committed, we may at the same time
see the cross on which Jesus Christ died and blotted out
this sentence by his blood, and so regain hope of pardon
and everlasting life.

Oh, how far more powerfully does the blood of Jesus
Christ speak for us, and obtain mercy for us from God,
than did the blood of Abel speak against Cain! *You have
come to Jesus the mediator of the New Testament, and to
the sprinkling of blood, which speaks better than that of
Abel.*3 As if the Apostle had said, "O sinners, happy
are you to be able, after you have sinned, to have recourse to Jesus crucified, who has shed all his blood, in
order to become the mediator of peace between sinners
and God, and to obtain pardon for them! Your iniquities cry out against you, but the blood of the Redeemer
pleads in your favor; and the divine justice cannot but
be appeased by the voice of this precious blood."

1 "Vere languores nostros ipse tulit, et dolores nostros ipse portavit."
Isa. 53.4.
2 "Delens quod adversus nos erat chirographum decreti, quod erat

contrarium nobis, et ipsum tulit de medio, affigens illud cruci." Col.
2.14.
3 "Accessistis ad ... Mediatorem Jesum, et sanguinis aspersio-
nem melius loquentem quam Abel." Heb. 12.22, 24.

[287] It is true that we shall have to render a rigorous
account to the Eternal Judge of all our sins. But who is
to be our Judge? *The Father has committed all judgment
to the Son.* 1 Let us comfort ourselves, the Eternal Father
has committed our judgment to our own Redeemer.
Therefore St. Paul encourages us, saying, *Who is he that
shall condemn? Christ Jesus who died, . . . who also makes
intercession for us.*2 Who is the judge to condemn us?
It is that same Savior who, in order not to condemn us
to everlasting death, vouchsafed himself to be condemned and to die; and not content with this, at this
moment intercedes with his Father for our salvation.
Hence St. Thomas of Villanova says: "What do you
fear, O sinner, if you detest your sin? How will he condemn you, who died in order not to condemn you? how
will he cast you from him, if you return to his feet, he
who came from heaven to seek you at the very time you
were flying from him?"3

And if we fear on account of our frailty to fall under
the assaults of our enemies, against whom we must continually wage war, behold what we have to do, as the
Apostle admonishes us: Let us run to the fight proposed
unto us: *looking on Jesus the author and finisher of faith,
who having joy proposed unto Him, underwent the cross,
despising the shame.*4 Let us go out to the battle with great
courage, looking at Jesus crucified, who from his cross
offers us his assistance, the victory, and crown. In past
times we fell into sin because we left off looking at the

1 "Pater . . . omne judicium dedit Filio." John 5.22.
2 Quis est qui condemnet? Christus Jesus, qui mortuus est, . . .
qui etiam interpellat pro nobis." Rom. 8.34.
3 "Quid times, peccator? Quomodo te damnabit poenitentem, qui
moritur ne damneris? Quomodo te abjiciet redeuntem, qui de coelo
venit quaerere te?" *Tr. de Adv. Dom.*
4 "Curramus ad propositum nobis certamen, aspicientes in Auc-
torem fidei et consummatorem Jesum, qui, proposito sibi gaudio,
sustinuit crucem, confusione contempta." Heb. 12.1,2.

[288] wounds and the pains endured by our Redeemer, and
so we did not have recourse to him for help. But if for
the future we set before our eyes all he has suffered for
love of us, and how he ever stands ready to assist us
when we have recourse to him, it is certain that we shall
not be conquered by our enemies. St. Teresa said, with
her wonted generosity, "I do not understand the fears
of certain persons, who say, The devil, the devil, so long
as we can say, God, God, and make Satan tremble."1
On the other hand, the saint assures us, that if we do
not place all our confidence in God, all our own exertions will be of little or no avail. "All our exertions,"
these are her own words, "are of little use, if we do not
give up entirely all trust in ourselves, and place it altogether in God."2 Oh, what two great mysteries of hope
and love for us are the Passion of Jesus Christ and the
Sacrament of the Altar! mysteries, which we could
have never believed, had not faith assured us of them.
That God Almighty should deign to become man, shed
all his blood, and die of sorrow upon a cross, and why?
To pay for our sins, and gain salvation for us rebellious
worms! And then his own very body, once sacrificed
upon the Cross for us, this he vouchsafes to give us for
our food, in order to become wholly united with us! O
God, how should not these two mysteries consume with

love the hearts of all men! And what sinner is there,
be he ever so abandoned, who can despair of pardon, if
he repent of the evil he has done, when he sees a God so
full of love for men, and so inclined to do them good?
Hence St. Bonaventure, full of confidence, said, "I will
have great confidence, firmly hoping that he who has
done and suffered so much for my salvation will deny
me nothing that I have need of."3 How can he refuse to

1 *Life*, ch. 25.
2 *Life*, ch. 8.
3 "Fiducialiter agam, immobiliter sperans nihil ad salutem necessarium ab eo negandum, qui tanta pro mea salute fecit et pertulit. "

[289] give me the graces necessary for my salvation, who
has done and suffered so much to save me?

Let us go therefore (the Apostle exhorts us) *with confidence
to the throne of grace, that we may obtain mercy, and find
grace in seasonable aid.*1 The throne of grace is the cross
on which Jesus sits to dispense graces and mercy to all
who come to him. But we must quickly have recourse
to him, if we would find seasonable aid for our salvation: for there will come a time perhaps when we shall
no longer be able to find it. Let us go quickly then and
embrace the cross of Jesus Christ, and let us go with
great confidence. Let us not be frightened by the sight
of our miseries; in Jesus crucified we shall find all riches,
all grace: *In all things you are made rich in Him, . . . so
that nothing is wanting to you in any grace.*2 The merits of
Jesus Christ have enriched us with all the divine treasures,
and have made us capable of every grace we can desire.

St. Leo says, "that Jesus has brought us by his death
more good than the devil has done us harm by sin."3

And by these words he explains what St. Paul said before him, that the gift of redemption is greater than sin : grace has overcome the offense. Not as the offense, so also is the gift : *where sin abounded, grace has abounded more.*4 From this the Savior encourages us to hope for every favor and every grace through his merits. And see how he teaches us the way to obtain all we want from his Eternal Father: *Amen, amen, I say to you, if you ask the Father*

1 "Adeamus ergo cum fiducia ad thronum gratiae, ut misericordiam consequamur, et gratiam inveniamus in auxilio opportune." Heb. 4.16.
2 "In omnibus divites facti estis in illo, . . . ita ut nihil vobis desit in ulla gratia." 1 Cor. 1.5,7.
3 "Ampliora adepti sumus per Christi gratiam, quam per diaboli amiseramus invidiam." *De Asc.* sermon 1.
4 "Non sicut delictum, ita et donum: . . . ubi abundavit delictum, superabundavit gratia." Rom. 5.15.

[290] *anything in My name, He will give it you?* 1 Whatever you desire, he says, ask for it of the Father in my name, and I promise you that you shall be heard. And indeed how shall the Father be able to deny us, when he has given us his only-begotten Son, whom he loves as himself? *He that spared not even His own Son, but delivered Him up for us all, how has He not also, with Him, given us all things?* 2 The Apostle says all things; so that no grace is excepted, neither pardon, nor perseverance, nor holy love, nor perfection, nor paradise, "all, all, he has given us." But we must pray to him. God is all liberality to those who call upon him: *Rich unto all that call upon Him.*3

I will again quote here many other beautiful thoughts of the Venerable John of Avila, which he has left us in his letters, on the great confidence we should have in the merits of Jesus Christ :

"Do not forget that Jesus Christ is the mediator between
the Eternal Father and ourselves; and that we are
beloved by him, and united to him by so strong bonds
of love that nothing can break them, so long as a man
does not himself dissolve them by some mortal sin. The
blood of Jesus cries out, and asks mercy for us; and
cries out so loudly that the noise of our sins is not heard.
The death of Jesus Christ has put to death our sins:
*O Death, I will be thy death!*4 Those who are lost are not
lost for lack of means of satisfaction, but because they
would not avail themselves of the sacraments as the
means of profiting by the satisfaction made by Jesus
Christ.

1 "Amen, amen, dico vobis: si quid petieritis Patrem in nomine
meo, dabit vobis." John 16.23.
2 "Pro nobis omnibus tradidit illum; quomodo non etiam cum illo
omnia nobis donavit?" Rom. 8.32.
3 "Dives in omnes qui invocant illum." Rom. 10.12.
4 "O mors! ero mors tua." Hosea 13.14.

[291] Jesus has taken upon himself the affair of remedying
our evils, as if it had been personally his own affair. So
that he has called our sins his own, although he did not
commit them, and has sought pardon for them; and with
the most tender love has prayed, as if he were praying
for himself, that all who should have recourse to him
might become objects of love. And as he sought, so he
found, because God has so ordained that Jesus and our
selves should be so united in one, that either he and we
should be loved, or he and we hated: and since Jesus is
not or cannot be hated, in the same way, if we remain
united by love to Jesus, we shall be also loved. By his
being loved by God, we are also loved, seeing that Jesus

Christ can do more to make us loved than we can do to make ourselves hated; since the Eternal Father loves Jesus Christ far more than he hates sinners.

Jesus said to his Father: *Father, I will that where I am, they also whom You have given Me may be with Me.*1 Love has conquered hatred; and thus we have been pardoned and loved, and are secure of never being abandoned, so strong is the tie of love that binds us. The Lord said by Isaiah: *Can a woman forget her infant? And if she should forget, yet will I not forget you. Behold, I have engraved you in My hands.*2 He has graven us in his hands with his own blood. Thus we should not trouble ourselves about anything, since everything is ordained by those hands which were nailed to the cross in testimony of the love he bears us.

Nothing can so trouble us on which Jesus Christ cannot reassure us. Let the sins I have committed surround me, let the devils lay snares for me, let fears for

1 "Pater! quos dedisti mihi, volo ut, ubi sum ego, et illi sint mecum." John 17.24.
2 "Numquid oblivisci potest mulier infantem suum, ut non misereatur filio uteri sui? et si illa oblita fuerit, ego tamen non obliviscar tui." Isa. 49.15.

[292] the future accuse me, by demanding mercy of the most tender Jesus Christ, who has loved me even until death, I cannot possibly lose confidence; for I see myself so highly valued, that God gave himself for me. O my Jesus, sure haven for those who seek You in time of peril! O most watchful Pastor, he deceives himself who does not trust in You, if only he has the will to amend his life! Therefore You have said: I am here, fear

not; I am he who afflicts and who consoles. Some from time to time I place in desolations, which seem equal to hell itself; but after a while I bring them out and console them. I am your advocate, who have made your cause my own. I am your surety, who am come to pay your debts. I am your Lord, who have redeemed you with my blood, not in order to abandon you, but to enrich you, having bought you at a great price. How shall I fly from him who seeks me, when I went forth to meet those who sought to outrage me? I did not turn away my face from him who struck me; and shall I from him who would adore me? How can my children doubt that I love them, seeing that out of love to them I placed myself in the hands of my enemies? Whom have I ever despised that loved me? Whom have I ever abandoned that sought my aid? Even I go seeking those that do not seek me."1

If you believe that the Eternal Father has given you his Son, believe also that he will give you everything else which is infinitely less than his Son. Do not think that Jesus Christ is forgetful of you, since he has left you, as the greatest memorial and pledge of his love, himself in the Most Holy Sacrament of the Altar.

Affections and Prayers

O my Jesus, my love, what joyful hope does Your Passion give me! How can I possibly fear not to receive from an Almighty

1 Part 2, *Letter* 48.

[293] God who has given me all his blood, the pardon of my sins, paradise, and all other graces that I require! Ah, my Jesus, my hope and my love, You, in order that I might not perish, did

give Your life; I love You above every good, my Redeemer and my God. You gave Yourself entirely to me; I give You my whole will, and with it I repeat that I love You, and I will always say, I love You, I love You. So I always desire to say in this life so I wish to die, breathing forth my last sigh with this dear word on my lips, My God, I love You; and from that moment I may commence a love towards You which shall last forever, and without cessation for all eternity. I love You, then; and be cause I love You, I repent above all things for having offended You. In order not to lose a passing satisfaction, I have been willing, wretch that l am, to lose You so often, O infinite good! This thought torments me more than any pain : but it is a consolation to me to think that I have to do with infinite goodness, that knows not how to despise a heart that truly loves. Oh, that I could die for You, who did die for me! My dear Redeemer, I surely hope of You eternal salvation in the life to come, and in this life I hope for holy perseverance in Your love; and there fore I propose always to ask it of You. And do You, by the merits of Your death, give me perse- verance in praying to You. This too I ask and hope of you, O Mary my Queen!

4.
How much we are obliged to love Jesus Christ

Jesus Christ as God has a claim on all our love; but
by the love which he has shown us, he wished to put us,
so to speak, under the necessity of loving him, at least
in gratitude for all that he has done and suffered for us.
He has greatly loved us, that we might love him greatly.
"Why does God love us, but that he may be loved?"1
wrote St. Bernard. And Moses had said the same before
him: *And now, Israel, what doth the Lord your God require*
of you, but that you fear the Lord your God . . . and love
*Him?*2

1 "Non ad aliud amat, nisi ut ametur." *On the Song of Songs,* sermon 83.

2 "Et nunc, Israel, quid Dominus Deus tuus petit a te, nisi ut timeas Dominum Deum tuum, . . . et diligas eum? Deut. 10.12.

[294] Therefore the first command which he gave us was this; *You shall love the Lord your God with Your whole heart.*1 And St. Paul says that love is the fulfilling of the law: *Love is the fulfilling of the law.*2 For "fulfilling" the Greek text has the "embracing of the law;"3 love embraces the entire law.

Who. indeed, at the sight of a crucified God dying for our love can refuse to love him? Those thorns, those nails, that cross, those wounds, and that blood, call upon us, and irresistibly urge us, to love him who has loved us so much. One heart is too little with which to love this God so enamored of us. In order to requite the love of Jesus Christ, it would require another God to die for his love. "Ah, why," exclaims St. Francis de Sales, "do we not throw ourselves on Jesus Christ, to die on the cross with him who was pleased to die there for the love of us?"4 The Apostle clearly impresses on us that Jesus Christ died for us for this end, that we might no longer live for ourselves, but solely for that God who died for us: *Christ died for all, that they also who live may not now live to themselves, but unto Him who died for them.*5

And the recommendation of Ecclesiasticus [Sirach] is here in point: *Forget not the kindness of your surety; for He has given His life for you.*6 Be not unmindful of him who has stood surety for you; who, to satisfy for your sins, was willing to pay off, by his death, the debt of punishment due from you. Oh, how desirous is Jesus Christ that we should continually remember his Passion! and

1 "Diliges Dominum Deum tuum ex toto corde tuo." Deut. 6.5.
2 "Plenitude legis est dilectio." Rom. 13.10.
3 "Completio legis."
4 *Love of God*, Bk. 7, ch. 8.
5 Pro omnibus mortuus est Christus, ut et qui vivunt, jam non sibi vivant, sed ei qui pro ipsis mortuus est." 2 Cor. 5.15.
6 "Gratiam fidejussoris ne obliviscaris; dedit enim pro te animam suam." Ecclus. (Sirach) 29.20.

[295] how it saddens him to see that we are so unmindful of it! Should a person endure for one of his friends insults, blows, and imprisonment, how afflicting would it be for him to know that that friend afterwards never gave it a thought, and cared not even to hear it spoken of! On the contrary, how gratified would he be to know that his friend constantly spoke of it with the warmest gratitude, and often thanked him for it. So it is pleasing to Jesus Christ when we preserve in our minds a grateful and loving recollection of the sorrows and death which he underwent for us. Jesus Christ was the desire of all the ancient Fathers; he was the desire of all nations before he was yet come upon earth. Now, how much more ought he to be our only desire and our only love, now that we know that he is really come, and are aware how much he has done and suffered for us, so that he even died upon the cross for love of us!

For this purpose he instituted the Sacrament of the Holy Eucharist on the day preceding his death, and gave us the injunction, that as often as we should be nourished with his most sacred flesh, we should be mindful of his death: *Take and eat; this is My body. . . . Do this In commemoration of Me, etch. For as often as you shall eat this bread and drink the chalice, you shall show the*

*death of the Lord until He come.*1 Wherefore the holy
Church prays:
"O God! who under this wonderful Sacrament have left
us a memorial of Your Passion,"2 etch. And she also
sings: "O sacred banquet, in which Christ is taken, the
memory of his Passion is renewed,"3 etc. Hence we may

1 "Accipite et manducate; hocest corpus meum: . . . hoc facite in
meam commemorationem. . . . Quotiescumque enim manducabitis
panem hunc, . . . mortem Domini annuntiabitis." 1 Cor. 11.24.
2 "Deus qui nobis sub Sacramento mirabili passionis tuae memoriam
reliquisti. . . ."
3 "O sacrum convivium, in quo Christus sumitur, recolitur memoria
passionis ejus. . ."

[296] gather how pleasing to Jesus Christ are they who
think frequently of his Passion, since it was for this very
purpose that he left himself in the holy Sacrament upon
our altars, in order that we might bear in continual and
grateful remembrance all that he suffered for us, and
by this means evermore increase our love towards
him. St. Francis de Sales called Mount Calvary the
mountain of lovers." It is impossible to remember that
mount and not love Jesus Christ, who died there for love
of us.

O God! and how is it that men do not love this God
who has done so much to be loved by men! Before the
Incarnation of the Word, man might have doubted
whether God loved him with a true love; but after the
coming of the Son of God, and after his dying for the
love of men, how can we possibly doubt of his love? "O
man," says St. Thomas of Villanova, "look on that cross,
on those torments, and that cruel death, which Jesus
Christ has suffered for you: after so great and so many
tokens of his love, you can no longer entertain a doubt

that he loves you, and loves you exceedingly." And St. Bernard says that "the cross and every wound of our Blessed Redeemer cry aloud to make us understand the love he bears us."1

In this grand mystery of man's redemption, we must consider how Jesus employed all his thoughts and zeal to discover every means of making himself loved by us. Had he merely wished to die for our salvation, it would have been sufficient had he been slain by Herod with the other children; but no, he chose before dying to lead, during thirty-three years, a life of hardship and suffer ing; and during that time, with a view to win our love, he appeared in several different guises. First of all, as a poor child born in a stable; then as a little boy helping

1 "Testis crux, testes dolores, testis amara mors quam pro te sustinuit." *Dom*. 17.

[297] in the workshop; and finally, as a criminal executed on a cross. But before dying on the cross, we see him in many different states, one and all calculated to excite our compassion, and to make himself loved: in agony in the garden, bathed from head to foot in a sweat of blood; afterwards, in the court of Pilate, torn with scourges; then treated as a mock king, with a reed in his hand, a ragged garment of purple on his shoulders, and a crown of thorns on his head; then dragged publicly through the streets to death, with the cross upon his shoulders; and at length, on the hill of Calvary, suspended on the cross by three iron nails. Tell me, does he merit our love or not, this God who has vouchsafed to endure all these torments, and to use so many means in order to captivate our love? Father John Rigouleux used to

say: "I would spend my life in weeping for love of a God whose love induced him to die for the salvation of men."

"Love is a great thing,"1 says St. Bernard. A great thing, a precious thing is love. Solomon, speaking of the divine wisdom, which is holy love, called it an infinite treasure; because he that possesses love is made partaker of the friendship of God: *For she is an infinite treasure to men, which they that use become the friends of God.*2

The angelic Doctor, St. Thomas, says that love is not only the queen of all virtues, but that, wherever she reigns, she draws along with her, as it were, in her train, all other virtues, and directs them all so as to bring us in closer union with God; but love is properly that which unites us with God. As St. Bernard tells us: "Charity is a virtue uniting us with God."3 And, indeed, it is over and over again signified in the holy

1 "Magna res amor." *On the Song of Songs,* sermon 83.
2 "Infinitus enim thesaurus est hominibus, quo qui usi sunt, participes facti sunt amicitiae Dei." Wisd. 7.14.
3 "Charitas est virtus conjungens nos Deo."

[298] Scriptures, that God loves whoever loves him: *I love them that love Me.*1 *If any one loves me . . . My Father will love Him; and We will come to him, and will make Our abode with him.*2 *He that abides in love abides in God, and God in him.*3 Behold the beautiful union which love produces; it unites the soul to God. Moreover, love supplies strength to practice and to suffer everything for God : *Love is strong as death.*4 St. Augustine writes: "Nothing is so hard that cannot be subdued by the fire

of love."5 Wherefore the saint says that where we love, either the labor is not felt, or if felt, the labor itself is loved: "In that which is loved, either there is no labor, or the labor is loved."6

Let us hear from St. John Chrysostom what are the effects of divine love in those souls in which it reigns : "When the love of God has taken possession of a soul, it produces an insatiable desire to work for the beloved; insomuch that however many and however vast the works which she does, and however prolonged the duration of her service, all seems nothing in her eyes, and she is afflicted at doing so little for God; and were it permitted her to die and consume herself for him, she would be most happy. Hence it is that she esteems herself an unprofitable servant in all that she does; because she is instructed by love to know what God deserves, and sees by this clear light all the defects of her actions, and finds in them motives for confusion and pain, well aware how mean is all that she can do for so great a Lord."

1 "Ego diligentes me diligo." Prov. 8.17.
2 "Si quis diligit me, . . . Pater meus diliget eum, et ad eum veniemus, et mansionem apud eum faciemus." John 14.23.
3 "Qui manet in charitate, in Deo manet, et Deus in eo." 1 John 4.16.
4 "Fortis est ut mors dilectio." Song of Songs, 8.6.
5 "Nihil tarm durum, quod amoris igne non vincatur." *De Mor. Eccl. cat.* ch. 22.
6 "In eo quod amatur, aut non laboratur, aut et labor amatur." *De Bono vid.* ch. 21.

[299] "Oh! how those persons delude themselves," says St. Francis de Sales, "who place virtue in anything else but in loving God! Some," writes the saint, "put perfection in austerities, others in alms, others in prayer, others in frequenting the holy sacraments. For my part,

I know of no other perfection than that of loving God with our whole heart; because all the other virtues, without love, are but a mere heap of stones. And if we do not perfectly enjoy this holy love, the fault lies with us, because we do not, once for all, come to the conclusion of giving up ourselves wholly to God."1

Our Lord said one day to St. Teresa, "Everything which does not give pleasure to me is vanity." Would that all understood well this great truth! *For the rest, one thing is necessary.*2 It is not necessary to be rich in this world, to gain the esteem of others, to lead a life of ease, to enjoy dignities, to have a reputation for learning; it is only necessary to love God and to do his will. For this single end has he created us, for this he preserves our life; and thus only can we gain admittance into Paradise. *Pitt me as a seal upon your heart, as a seal upon your arm.*3 The Lord thus speaks to all his espoused souls. Put me as a seal upon your heart and upon your arm, in order that all your desires and actions may tend to me; upon your heart, that no other love but mine may enter there upon your arm, in order that all you do may have me for its sole object. Oh, how quickly does that soul speed onwards to perfection, that in all its actions regards but Jesus crucified, and has no other pretension than to gratify him!

To acquire, then, a true love of Jesus Christ should be our only care. The masters of spiritual life describe the

1 *Spirit of St Francis de Sales*, Pt. 1, ch. 25.
2 "Porro unum est necessarium." Luke 10.42.
3 "Pone me ut signaculum super cor tuum, ut signaculum super brachium tuum." Song of Songs, 8.6.

[300] marks of true love. Love, say they, is fearful, and its fear is none other than that of displeasing God. It is generous, because, trusting in God, it is never daunted even at the greatest enterprises for his glory, It is strong, because it subdues all its evil appetites, even in the midst of the most violent temptations, and of the darkest desolations. It is obedient, because it immediately flies to execute the divine will. It is pure, because it loves God alone, and for the sole reason that he deserves to be loved. It is ardent, because it would inflame all man kind, and willingly see them consumed with divine love. It is inebriating, for it causes the soul to live as it were out of itself, as if it no longer saw, nor felt, nor had any more senses left for earthly things, bent wholly on loving God. It is unitive, by producing a strict union between the will of the creature and the will of the Creator. It is longing, for it fills the soul with desires of leaving this world, to fly and unite itself perfectly with God in its true and happy country, where it may love him with all its strength.

But no one teaches us so well the real characteristics and practice of love as the great preacher of love, St. Paul. In his first epistle to the Corinthians, he says, in the first place, that without love man is nothing, and that nothing profits him: *If I should have all faith, so that I could remove mountains, and have not love, I am nothing. And if I should distribute all my goods to feed the poor, and if I should deliver my body to be burned, and have not love, it profits me nothing,*1 So that even should a person have faith strong enough to remove mountains, like St. Gregory Thaumaturgus, but had not love, it would

1 "Et si habuero omnem fidem, ita ut montes transferam, charitatem autem non habuero, nihil sum. Et si distribuero in cibos pauperum

omnes facultates meas; et si tradidero corpus meum, ita ut ardeam, charitatem autem non habuero, nihil mihi prodest." 1 Cor. 13.2, 3.

[301] profit him nothing. Should he give all his goods to the poor, and even willingly suffer martyrdom, but remain void of charity, should he do it, that is, for any other end than that of pleasing God, it would profit him nothing at all. Then St. Paul gives us the marks of true love, and at the same time teaches us the practice of those virtues which are the daughters of love; and he goes on to say : *Charity is patient, is kind; love envies not, deals not perversely; is not puffed up, is not ambitious; seeks not her own; is not provoked to anger, thinks no evil; rejoices not in iniquity, but rejoices with the truth; bears all things, believes all things, hopes all things, endures all things.*1

Let us therefore, in the present book, proceed to consider these holy practices, that we may thus see if the love which we owe to Jesus Christ truly reigns within us; as likewise that we may understand in what virtues we should chiefly exercise ourselves, in order to persevere and advance in this holy love.

Affections and Prayers

most lovely and most loving Heart of Jesus, miserable is the heart which does not love You! O God, for the love of men You did die on the cross, helpless and forsaken, and how then can men live so forgetful of You? O love of God! O ingratitude of man! O men, O men! do but cast one look on the innocent Son of God, agonizing on the cross, and dying for you, in order to satisfy the divine justice for your sins, and by this means to allure you to love him. Observe how, at the same time, he prays his eternal Father to forgive you. Behold him, and love him. Ah, my Jesus, how small is the number of those that love You! Wretched too am I; for I also have lived so

1 "Charitas patiens est, benigna est; charitas non aemulatur, non agit perperam, non inflatur, non est ambitiosa, non quaerit quae sua sunt, non irritatur; non cogitat malum, non gaudet super iniquitate, con-gaudet autem veritati; omnia suffert, omnia credit, omnia sperat, omnia sustinet." 1 Cor. 13.4-7.

[302] many years unmindful of You, and have grievously offended You, my beloved Redeemer! It is not so much the punishment I have deserved that makes me weep, as the love which You have borne me. O sorrows of Jesus! O outrages of Jesus! O wounds of Jesus! O death of Jesus! O love of Jesus! rest deeply engraved in my heart, and may your sweet recollection be forever fixed there, to wound me and inflame me continually with love. I love You, my Jesus; I love You, my sovereign good; I love You, my love and my all; I love You, and I will love You forever. Oh, permit me never more to forsake You, never more to lose You! Make me entirely Yours; do so by the merits of Your death. In this I firmly trust.

And I have a great confidence also in your intercession, O Mary, my Queen; make me love Jesus Christ and make me also love you, my Mother and my hope!

"Si quis non amat Dominum nostrum Jesum Christum, sit anathema!"
"If any man love not our Lord Jesus Christ, let him be anathema!" 1 Cor. 16.22.

"Charitas patiens est, benigna est; charitas non aemulatur, non agit perperam, non inflatur, non est ambitiosa, non

quaerit quae sua sunt, non irritatur; non cogitat malum, non gaudet super iniquitate, congaudet autem veritati; omnia suffert, omnia credit, omnia sperat, omnia sustinet." "Love is patient, is kind; love envies not, deals not perversely, is not puffed up, is not ambitious, seeks not her own, is not provoked to anger; thinks no evil, rejoices not in iniquity, but rejoices with the truth; bears all things, believes all things, endures all things." (1 Cor. 13.4-7)

Practice of the love of Jesus Christ

CHAPTER 1

LOVE IS PATIENT
(Charitas patiens est. 1 Cor. 13.4)

He that loves Jesus Christ loves Sufferings

THIS earth is the place for meriting, and therefore it is a place for suffering. Our true country, where God has prepared for us repose in everlasting joy, is paradise. We have but a short time to stay in this world; but in this short time we have many labors to undergo: *Man born of a woman, living for a short time, is filled with many miseries.*1 We must suffer, and all must suffer; be they just, or be they sinners, each one must carry his cross. He that carries it with patience is saved; he that carries it with impatience is lost. St. Augustine says, the same miseries send some to paradise and some to hell: "One and the same blow lifts the good to glory, and reduces the bad to ashes."2 The same saint observes, that by the test of suffering the chaff in the Church of God is distinguished from the wheat : he that humbles himself under tribulations, and is resigned to the will of God, is wheat for paradise; he that grows haughty and is enraged, and so forsakes God, is chaff for hell.

On the day when the cause of our salvation shall be

1 "Homo natus de muliere, brevi vivens tempore, repletur multis miseriis." Job 14.1.
2 "Una eademque tunsio bonos producit ad gloriam, malos redigit in favillam." *Sermon* 52.

[306] decided, our life must be found conformable to the life of Jesus Christ, if we would enjoy the happy sentence of the predestined: *For whom He foreknew He also predestined to be made conformable to the image of His Son.*1 This was the end for which the Eternal Word descended upon earth, to teach us, by his example, to carry with patience the cross which God sends us: *Christ suffered for us* (wrote St. Peter), *leaving you an example, that you should follow His steps.*2 So that Jesus Christ suffered on purpose to encourage us to suffer. O God! what a life was that of Jesus Christ! A life of ignominy and pain. The Prophet calls our Redeemer *despised, and the most abject of men, a man of sorrows.*3 A man held in contempt, and treated as the lowest, the vilest among men, a man of sorrows; yes, for the life of Jesus Christ was made up of hardships and afflictions.

Now, in the same manner as God has treated his beloved Son, so does he treat every one whom he loves, and whom he receives for his son: *For whom the Lord loves He chastises; and He scourges every son whom He receives.*4

For this reason he one day said to St. Teresa: "Know that the souls dearest to my Father are those who are afflicted with the greatest sufferings."5 Hence the saint said of all her troubles, that she would not exchange them for all the treasures in the world. She appeared after her death to a soul, and revealed to her that she enjoyed an immense reward in heaven, not so much for her good works, as for the sufferings which she cheerfully bore in this life for the love of God; and that if she

1 "Nam quos praescivit, et praedestinavit conformes fieri imaginis Filii sui." Rom. 8.29.

2 "Christus passus est pro nobis, vobis relinquens exemplum, ut sequamini vestigia ejus." 1 Pet. 2.21.

3 "Despectum et novissimum virorum." Isa. 53.3.

4 "Quem enim diligit Dominus, castigat; flagellat autem omnem filium quem recipit." Heb. 12.6.

5 *Life*, additions.

[307] could possibly entertain a wish to return upon earth, the only reason would be in order that she might suffer more
for God.

He that loves God in suffering earns a double reward in paradise. St. Vincent de Paul 1 said that it was a great misfortune to be free from suffering in this life. And he added, that a congregation or an individual that does not suffer, and is applauded by all the world, is not far from a fall. It was on this account that St. Francis of Assisi, on the day that he had suffered nothing for God, became afraid lest God had forgotten him. St. John Chrysostom 2 says that when God endows a man with the grace of suffering, he gives him a greater grace than that of raising the dead to life; because in performing miracles man remains God's debtor; whereas in suffering, God makes himself the debtor of man. And he adds,3 that whoever endures something for God, even had he no other gift than the strength to suffer for the God whom he loves, this would procure for him an immense reward. Wherefore he affirmed, that he considered St. Paul to have received a greater grace in being bound in chains for Jesus Christ, than in being rapt to the third heaven in ecstasy.

*But patience has a perfect work.*4 The meaning of this is, that nothing is more pleasing to God than to see a soul suffering with patience all the crosses sent it by him. The effect of love is to liken the lover to the person loved. St. Francis de Sales said, "All the wounds of Christ are so many mouths, which preach to us that we must suffer for him. The science of the saints is to suffer constantly for Jesus; and in this way we shall soon become saints." A person that loves Jesus Christ is anxious to be treated like Jesus Christ, poor, persecuted, and despised. St. John beheld all the saints clothed in

1 *Abelly*, Bk. 3, ch. 43.
2 *In Phil.* hom. 4.
3 *In Eph.* hom. 8.
4 "Patientia autem opus perfectum habet." James 1.4.

[308] white, and with palms in their hands: *Clothed with white robes, and palms in their hands.*1 The palm is the symbol of martyrs, and yet all the saints did not suffer martyr dom; why, then, do all the saints bear palms in their hands? St. Gregory replies, that all the saints have been martyrs either of the sword or of patience; so that, he adds, "we can be martyrs without the sword, if we keep patience."2

The merit of a soul that loves Jesus Christ consists in loving and in suffering. Hear what our Lord said to St. Teresa: "Think you, my child, that merit consists in enjoyment? No, it consists in suffering and in loving. Look at my life, wholly embittered with afflictions. Be assured, my child, that the more my Father loves any one, the more sufferings he sends him; they are the standard of his love. Look at my wounds; your torments will never reach so far. It is absurd to suppose that my Father favors with his friendship those who are strangers to suffering."3 And for our consolation St. Teresa makes this remark: "God never sends a trial, but he immediately rewards it with some favor."4 One day Jesus Christ appeared to the blessed Baptista Varani,5 and told her of three special favors which he will often bestow on cherished souls: the first is, not to sin; the second, which is greater, to perform good works; the third, and the greatest of all, to suffer for his love. So that St. Teresa 6 used to say, whenever any one does something for God, the Almighty repays him with some trial And therefore the saints, on receiving tribulations,

1 "Amicti stolis albis, et palmae in manibus eorum." Apoc. (Rev.) 7.9.
2 "Nos sine ferro esse possumus martyres, si patientiam veraciter in animo custodimus." *In Evang.* hom. 35.
3 *Life*, additions.
4 *Life*, ch. 30.
5 *Boll.* 31 *Maii. Vit.* ch. 7.
6 *Foundations*, ch. 31.

[309] thanked God for them. St. Louis of France, referring to his captivity in Turkey, said: "I rejoice, and thank God more for the patience which he accorded me in the time of my imprisonment, than if he had made me master of the universe." And when St. Elizabeth, princess of Thuringia, after her husband's death, was banished with her son from the kingdom, and found herself homeless and abandoned by all, she went to a convent of the Franciscans, and there had the Te Deum sung in thanks giving to God for tiie signal favor of being allowed to suffer for his love.

St. Joseph Calasanctius used to say, "All suffering is slight to gain heaven." And the Apostle had already said the same: *The sufferings of this time are not worthy to be compared with the glory to come, that shall be revealed in us.*1

It would be a great gain for us to endure all the torments of all the martyrs during our whole lives, in order to enjoy one single moment of the bliss of paradise; with what readiness, then, should we embrace our crosses, when we know that the sufferings of this transitory life will gain for us an everlasting beatitude! *That which is at present momentary and light of our tribulation, works for us above measure exceedingly an eternal weight of glory.*2 St. Agapitus, while still a mere boy in years, was threatened by the tyrant to have his head covered with a red-hot helmet; on which he replied, "And what better fortune could possibly befall me, than to lose my head here, to have it crowned hereafter in heaven?" This made St. Francis exclaim :

"I look for such a meed of bliss,
That all my pains seem happiness."

1 "Non sunt condignae passiones hujus temporis ad futuram gloriam quae revelabitur in nobis." Rom. 8.18.
2 "Momentaneum et leve tribulationis nostrae supra modum in sublimitate aeternum gloriae pondus operatur in nobis." 2 Cor. 4.17.

[310] But whoever desires the crown of paradise must undergo combat and suffering: If we suffer, we shall also reign.1 We cannot get a reward without merit; and no merit is to be had without patience: *He is not crowned, except he strive lawfully.* 2 And the person that strives with the greatest patience shall have the greatest reward. Wonderful in deed! When the temporal goods of this world are in question, worldlings endeavor to procure as much as they can; but when it is a question of the goods of eternal life, they say, "It is enough if we get a little corner in heaven!" Such is not the language of the saints: they are satisfied with anything whatever in this life,

even more, they strip themselves of all earthly goods; but concerning eternal goods, they strive to obtain them in as large a measure as possible. I would ask which of the two act with more wisdom and prudence?

But even with regard to the present life, it is certain that he who suffers with most patience enjoys the greatest peace. It was a saying of St. Philip Neri,3 that in this world there is no purgatory; it is either all paradise or all hell: he that patiently supports tribulations enjoys a paradise; he that does not do so, suffers a hell. Yes, for (as St. Teresa writes) he that embraces the crosses sent him by God feels them not. St. Francis de Sales, finding himself on one occasion beset on every side with tribulations, said, "For some time back the severe oppositions and secret contrarieties which have befallen me afford me so sweet a peace, that nothing can equal it; and they give me such an assurance that my soul will ere long be firmly united with God, that I can say with all truth that they are the sole ambition, the sole desire of my heart."4

1 "Si sustinebimus, et conregnabimus." 2 Tim. 2.12.
2 "Qui certat in agone, non coronatur, nisi legitime certaverit."
 2 Tim. 2.5.
3 Bacci, Bk. 2, ch. 20.
4 *Spirit of St Francis de Sales*, ch. 19.

[311] And indeed peace can never be found by one who leads an irregular life, but only by him who lives in union with God and with his blessed will. A certain missionary of a religious Order, while in the Indies, was one day standing to witness the execution of a person under sentence of death, and already on the scaffold: the criminal called the missionary to him, and said, "You

must know, Father, that I was once a member of your
Order; while I observed the rules I led a very happy life;
but when, afterwards, I began to relax in the strict observ-
ance of them, I immediately experienced pain in everything;
so much so, that I abandoned the religious life, and gave
myself up to vice, which has finally reduced me to the
melancholy pass in which you at present behold me."
And in conclusion he said, "I tell you this, that my example may be a warning to others." The Venerable Father
Louis da Ponte said, "Take the sweet things of this life
for bitter, and the bitter for sweet; and so you will be
in the constant enjoyment of peace. Yes, for though the
sweet are pleasant to sense, they invariably leave behind
them the bitterness of remorse of conscience, on account
of the imperfect satisfaction which, for the most part,
they afford; but the bitter, when taken with patience from
the hand of God, become sweet, and dear to the souls
who love him."

Let us be convinced that in this valley of tears true
peace of heart cannot be found, except by him who endures and lovingly embraces sufferings to please Almighty God: this is the consequence of that corruption
in which all are placed through the infection of sin. The
condition of the saints on earth is to suffer and to love;
the condition of the saints in heaven is to enjoy and to
love. Father Paul Segneri the younger, in a letter
which he wrote one of his penitents to encourage her to
suffer, gave her the counsel to keep these words inscribed
at the foot of her crucifix: "It is thus how one loves." It is
[312] not simply by suffering, but by desiring to suffer for
the love of Jesus Christ, that a soul gives the surest signs
of really loving him. And what greater acquisition (said
St. Teresa) can we possibly make than to have some token
of gratifying Almighty God?1 Alas, how ready are the

greatest part of men to take alarm at the bare mention of crosses, of humiliations, and of afflictions! Nevertheless, there are many souls who find all their delight in suffering, and who would be quite disconsolate did they pass their time on this earth without suffering. The sight of Jesus crucified (said a devout person) renders the cross so lovely to me, that it seems to me I could never be happy without suffering; the love of Jesus Christ is sufficient for me for all. Listen how Jesus advises every one who would follow him to take up and carry his cross: *Let him take up his cross, and follow Me.*2 But we must take it up and carry it, not by constraint and against our will, but with humility, patience, and love.

Oh, how acceptable to God is he that humbly and patiently embraces the crosses which he sends him! St. Ignatius of Loyola said, "There is no wood so apt to enkindle and maintain love towards God as the wood of the cross;" that is, to love him in the midst of sufferings. One day St. Gertrude asked our Lord what she could offer him most acceptable, and he replied, "My child, you can do nothing more gratifying- to me than to submit patiently to all the tribulations that befall you." Wherefore the great servant of God, Sister Victoria Angelini, affirmed that one day of crucifixion was worth a hundred years of all other spiritual exercises. And the Venerable Father John of Avila said, "One blessed be God in contrarieties is worth more than a thousand thanksgivings in prosperity." Alas, how little men know of the inestimable value of afflictions endured for God!

1 *Life*, ch. 10.
2 "Tollat crucem suam quotidie, et sequatur me." Luke 9.23.

[313] The Blessed Angela of Foligno said, "that if we knew the just value of suffering for God, it would become an object of plunder;" which is as much as to say, that each one would seek an opportunity of robbing his neighbor of the occasions of suffering. For this reason St. Mary Magdalene de Pazzi, well aware as she was of the merit of sufferings, sighed to have her life prolonged rather than to die and go to Heaven, "because," said she, "in Heaven one can suffer no more."

A soul that loves God has no other end in view but to be wholly united with him; but let us learn from St. Catherine of Genoa what is necessary to be done to arrive at this perfect union: "To attain union with God, adversities are indispensable; because by them God aims at destroying all our corrupt propensities within and without. And hence all injuries, contempts, infirmities, abandonment of relatives and friends, con - fusions, temptations, and other mortifications, all are in the highest degree necessary for us, in order that we may carry on the fight, until by repeated victories we come to extinguish within us all vicious movements, so that they are no longer felt; and we shall never arrive at divine union until adversities, instead of seeming bitter to us, become all sweet for God s sake."

It follows, then, that a soul that sincerely desires to belong to God must be resolved, as St. John of the Cross 1 writes, not to seek enjoyments in this life, but to suffer in all things; she must embrace with eagerness all voluntary mortifications, and with still greater eager ness those which are involuntary, since they are the more welcome to Almighty God.

*The patient man is better than the valiant.*2 God is pleased with a person who practices mortification by fasting, hair-cloths, and disciplines, on account of the courage

1 *Ascent of Mount Carmel*, Bk. 2, ch. 7.
2 "Melior est patiens viro forti." Prov. 16.32.

[314] displayed in such mortifications; but he is much more pleased with those who have the courage to bear patiently and gladly such crosses as come from his own divine hand. St. Francis de Sales said, "Such mortifications as come to us from the hand of God, or from men by his permission, are always more precious than those which are the offspring of our own will; for it is a general rule, that wherever there is less of our own choice, God is better pleased, and we ourselves derive greater profit."1 St. Teresa taught the same thing: "We gain more in one day by the oppositions which come to us from God or our neighbor than by ten years of mortifications of self-infliction."2 Wherefore St. Mary Magdalene de Pazzi made the generous declaration, that there could not be found in the whole world an affliction so severe, but what she would gladly bear with the thought that it came from God; and, in fact, during the five years of severe trial which the saint underwent, it was enough to restore peace to her soul to remember that it was by the will of God that she so suffered. Ah, God, that infinite treasure is cheaply purchased at any cost! Father Hippolytus Durazzo used to say, "Purchase God at what cost you will, he can never be dear."

Let us then beseech God to make us worthy of his love; for if we did but once perfectly love him, all the goods of this earth would seem to us but as smoke and dirt, and we should relish disgraces and afflictions as delights. Let us hear what St. John Chrysostom says of a soul wholly given up to Almighty God: "He who has attained the perfect love of God seems to be alone on the earth, he no longer cares either for glory or disgrace, he scorns temptations and afflictions, he loses all relish and appetite for created things. And as noth- ing in this world brings him any support or repose, he

1 *Spirit of St Francis de Sales*, ch. 4.
2 *Way of Perfection*, ch. 37.

[315] goes incessantly in search of his beloved without ever feeling wearied; so that when he toils, when he eats, when he is watching, or when sleeping, in every action and word, all his thoughts and desires are fixed upon finding his beloved; because his heart is where his treasure is."*

Affections and Prayers

My dear and beloved Jesus, my treasure, I have deserved by my offenses never more to be allowed to love You; but by Your merits, I entreat You, make me worthy of Your pure love.1 love You above all things; and I repent with my whole heart, of having ever despised You, and driven You from my soul; but now I love You more than myself; I love You with all my heart, O infinite good! I love You, I love You, I love You, and I have not a wish besides that of loving You perfectly; nor have I a fear besides that of ever seeing myself deprived of Your love. O my most loving Redeemer, enable me to know how great a good You are, and how great is the love You have borne me in order to oblige me to love You! Ah, my God, permit me not to live any longer unmindful of so much good ness! Enough have I offended You, I will never leave You again; I wish to employ all the remainder of my days in loving You, and in pleasing You. My Jesus, my Love, lend me

Your aid; help a sinner who wishes to love You and to be wholly Your own.

O Mary my hope, your Son hears you; pray to him in my behalf, and obtain for me the grace of loving him perfectly!

* In this chapter we have spoken of patience in general; in Chapter 10 we shall treat more particularly of occasions in which we have especially to practice patience.

CHAPTER 2

LOVE IS KIND
(Charitas benigna est)

He that loves Jesus Christ loves Meekness

[316] THE spirit of meekness is peculiar to God: *My spirit is sweet above honey.*1 Hence it is that a soul that loves God loves also all those whom God loves, namely, her neighbors; so that she eagerly seeks every occasion of helping all, of consoling all, and of making all happy as far as she can. St. Francis de Sales, who was the master and model of holy meekness, says, "Humble meekness is the virtue of virtues, which God has so much recommended to us; therefore we should endeavor to practice it always and in all things."2 Hence the saint gives us this rule: "What you see can be done with love, do it; and what you see cannot be done without offense, leave it un-done."3 He means, when it can be omitted without offending God; because an offense of God must always, and as quickly as possible, be prevented by him who is bound to prevent it.

This meekness should be particularly observed towards the poor, who, by reason of their poverty, are often harshly treated by men. It should likewise be especially practiced towards the sick who are suffering under infirmities, and for the most part meet with small help from others. Meek-ness is more especially to be observed in our behavior towards enemies: *Overcome evil with good.*4 Hatred must

1 "Spiritus enim meus super mel dulcis." Ecclus. (Sirach) 24.27.
2 *Letter* 853.
3 *Letter* 786.

4 "Vince in bono malum." Rom. 12.21.

[317] be overcome by love, and persecution by meekness; thus the saints acted, and so they conciliated the affections of their most exasperated enemies.

"There is nothing," says St. Francis de Sales, "that gives so much edification to our neighbor as meekness of behavior."1 The saint, therefore, was generally seen smiling, and with a countenance beaming with love, which gave a tone to all his words and actions. This gave occasion to St. Vincent de Paul 2 to declare that he never knew a kinder man in his life. He said further, that it seemed to him that in St Francis de Sales was a true likeness of Jesus Christ. Even in refusing what he could not in conscience comply with, he did so with such sweetness, that all, though unsuccessful in their requests, went away satisfied and well-disposed towards him. He was gentle towards all, towards Superiors, towards equals and inferiors, at home and abroad; in contrast with some, who, as the saint used to say, "seemed angels abroad, but were devils at home."3 Moreover, the saint, in his conduct towards servants, never complained of their remissness; at most he would give them an admonition, but always in the gentlest terms. And this is a thing most praiseworthy in Superiors.

The Superior should use all kindness towards those under him. When telling them what they have to do, he should rather request than command. St. Vincent de Paul said: "A Superior will never find a better means of being readily obeyed than meekness." And to the same effect was the saying of St. Jane Frances of Chantal: "I have tried various methods of governing, but I have not found any better than that of meekness and forbearance."4

And more than this, the Superior should be kind even
in the correction of faults. It is one thing to correct

1 *Letter* 605
2 *Abelly*, Bk. 3, ch. 27.
3 *Introduction to the Devout Life.*, ch. 3.
4. *Mem. de la M. de Chaugy*, Pt. 3, ch. 19.

[318] with firmness, and another with harshness; it is needful at times to correct with firmness, when .the fault is serious, and especially if it be repeated after the subject has
already been admonished of it; but let us always be on
our guard against harsh and angry correction; he that
corrects with anger does more harm than good. This is
that bitter zeal reproved by St. James. Some make a
boast of keeping their family in order by severity, and
they say it is the only successful method of treatment;
but St. James speaks not so: *But if you have bitter zeal
.... glory not.*1 If on some rare occasion it be necessary to speak a cross word, in order to bring the offender
to a proper sense of his fault, yet in the end we ought
invariably to leave him with a gentle countenance and a
word of kindness. Wounds must be healed after the
fashion of the good Samaritan in the Gospel, with wine
and oil: "But as oil," said St. Francis de Sales, "always
swims on the surface of all other liquors, so must meek
ness prevail over all our actions." And when it occurs
that the person under correction is agitated, then the
reprehension must be deferred till his anger has subsided, or else we should only increase his indignation.
The Canon Regular St. John said: "When the house is
on fire, one must not cast wood into the flames."

*You know not of what spirit you are.*2 Such were the
words of Jesus Christ to his disciples James and John,

when they would have brought down chastisements on
the Samaritans for expelling them from their country.
Ah, said the Lord to them, and what spirit is this? this
is not my spirit, which is sweet and gentle; for I am
come not to destroy but to save souls: *The Son of Man
came not to destroy souls, but to save.*3 And would you in-

1 "Quod si zelum amarum habetis, . . . nolite gloriari." James 3.14.
2 "Nescitis cujus spiritus estis." Luke 9.55.
3 "Filius hominis non venit animas perdere, sed salvare." Luke
10.56.

[319] induce me to destroy them? Oh, hush! and never
make such a request to me, for such is not according to
my spirit. And, in fact, with what meekness did Jesus
Christ treat the adulteress! *Woman, said He, has no man
condemned you? Neither will I condemn you! Go, and
now sin no more.*1 He was satisfied with merely warning
her not to sin again, and sent her away in peace. With
what meekness, again, did he seek the conversion of the
Samaritan woman, and so, in fact, converted her! He
first asked her to give him to drink; then he said to her:
If you did know who He is that says to you, Give me to
drink! and then he revealed to her that he was the ex-
pected Messiah. And, again, with what meekness did
he strive to convert the impious Judas, admitting him to
eat of the same dish with him, washing his feet and ad-
monishing him in the very act of his betrayal: Judas, and
do you thus betray me with a kiss? *Judas, do you betray
the Son of Man with a kiss?*2 And see how he converted
Peter after his denial of him! *And the Lord turning,
looked on Peter.*3 On leaving the house of the high-priest,
without making him a single reproach, he cast on him a
look of tenderness, and thus converted him; and so effectually did he convert him, that during his whole life

long Peter never ceased to bewail the injury he had
done to his Master.

Oh, how much more is to be gained by meekness than
by harshness! St. Francis de Sales said there was nothing more bitter than the bitter almond, but if made into
a preserve, it becomes sweet and agreeable: thus corrections, though in their nature very unpleasant, are ren-
dered pleasant by love and meekness, and so are attended
with more beneficial results. St. Vincent de Paul said

1 "Mulier, . . . nemo te condemnavit? . . . Nec ego te condemnabo.
Vade, et jam amplius noli peccare." John 8.10,11.
2 "Juda! osculo Filium hominis tradis?" Luke 22.48.
3 "Conversus Dominus respexit Petrum." Luke 22.61.

[320] of himself, that in the government of his own congregation he had never corrected any one with severity, except
on three occasions, when he supposed there was reason
to do so, but that he regretted it ever afterwards, because
he found it turned out badly; whereas he had always admirably succeeded by gentle correction.1

St. Francis de Sales obtained from others whatever he
wished by his meek behavior; and by this means he
managed to gain the most hardened sinners to God. It
was the same with St. Vincent de Paul, who taught his
disciples this maxim : "Affability, love, and humility have
a wonderful efficacy in winning the hearts of men, and
in prevailing on them to undertake things most repug-
nant to nature." He once gave a great sinner to the care
of one of his Fathers, to bring him to sentiments of true
repentance; but that Father, in spite of all his endeavors,
found his labor fruitless, so that he begged the saint to
speak a word to him. The saint accordingly spoke with

him, and converted him. That sinner subsequently declared that the singular sweetness of Father Vincent had worked upon his heart. Wherefore it was that the saint could not bear his missionaries to treat sinners with severity; and he told them that the infernal spirit took advantage of the strictness of some to work the greater ruin of souls.

Kindness should be observed towards all on all occasions and at all times. St. Bernard remarks,2 that certain persons are gentle as long as things fall out to their taste; but scarcely do they experience some opposition or contradiction than they are instantly on fire, like Mount Vesuvius itself. Such as these may be called burning coals, but hidden under the embers. Whoever would become a saint, must, during this life, resemble the lily among thorns, which, however much it may be

1 *Abelly*, Bk. 3, ch. 27.
2 *In Adv. Domini*, sermon 4.

[321] pricked by them, never ceases to be a lily; that is, it is always equally sweet and serene. The soul that loves God maintains an imperturbable peace of heart; and she shows this in her very countenance, being ever mistress of herself, alike in prosperity and adversity, according to the lines of Cardinal Petrucci:

"Of outward things he views the varying guise,
While in his soul's most inmost depth
Undimmed God's image lies."

Adversity brings out a person's real character. St. Francis de Sales very tenderly loved the Order of the Visitation, which had cost him so much labor. He saw it several times in imminent danger of dissolution on account of the persecutions it underwent; but the saint never for a moment lost his peace, and was ready, if such was the will of God, to see it entirely destroyed; and then it was that he said: "For some time back the trying oppositions and secret adversities which have befallen me afford me so sweet a peace, that nothing can equal it; and they give me such an earnest of the immediate union of my soul with God, that, in truth, they form the sole desire of my heart."1

Whenever it happens that we have to reply to some one who insults us, let us be careful to answer with meekness: *A mild answer dissolves wrath.*2 A mild reply is enough to quench every spark of anger. And in case we feel irritated, it is best to keep silence, because then it seems only just to give vent to all that rises to our lips; but when our passion has subsided, we shall see that all our words were full of faults.

And when it happens that we ourselves commit some fault, we must also practice meekness in our own regard. To be exasperated at ourselves after a fault is not humility, but a subtle pride, as if we were anything else than

1 *Spirit of St Francis de Sales*, ch. 10.
2 "Responsio mollis frangit iram." Prov. 15.1.

[322] the weak and miserable things that we are. St. Teresa said: "The humility that disturbs does not come from God, but from the devil."1 To be angry at ourselves after the commission of a fault is a fault worse than the one committed, and will be the occasion of many other faults; it will make us leave off our devotions, prayers, and communions; or if we do practice them, they will be done

very badly. St. Aloysius Gonzaga said that we cannot
see in troubled waters, and that the devil fishes in them.
A soul that is troubled knows little of God and of what
it ought to do. Whenever, therefore, we fall into any
fault, we should turn to God with humility and confidence, and craving his forgiveness, say to him, with St.
Catherine of Genoa: "O Lord, this is the produce of
my own garden! I love You with my whole heart, and
I repent of the displeasure I have given You! I will
never do the like again: grant me Your assistance!"

Affections and Prayers

O blessed chains that bind the soul with God, oh, enfold me
still closer, and in links so firm that I may never be able to
loosen myself from the love of my God! My Jesus, I love You;
O treasure, O life of my soul, to You I cling, and I give myself
wholly unto You! No, indeed, my beloved Lord, I wish never
more to cease to love You. You who, to atone for my sins,
did allow Yourself to be bound as a criminal, and so bound to
be led to death through the streets of Jerusalem, You who did
consent to be nailed to the cross, and did not leave it until
life itself had left You, oh, permit me never to be separated
from You again; I regret above every other evil, to have at one
time turned my back upon You, and henceforth I resolve by
Your grace to die rather than to give You the slightest displeasure. O my Jesus, I abandon myself to You. I love You
with my whole heart; I love You more than myself. I have
offended You in times past; but now I bitterly repent of it, and
I would willingly die of grief. Oh, draw me entirely to Yourself!

1 *Life*, ch. 30.

[323] I renounce all sensible consolations; I wish for You alone,
and nothing more. Make me love You, and then do with me
what you will.

O Mary, my hope, bind me to Jesus; and grant me to live and die in union with him, in order to come one day to the happy kingdom, where I shall have no more fear of ever being separated from his love!

CHAPTER 3

LOVE DOES NOT ENVY
(*Charitas non aemulatur*)

**The Soul that loves Jesus Christ does not envy the
Great Ones of this World, but only those who are
Greater Lovers of Jesus Christ**

ST. GREGORY explains this next characteristic of charity in saying, that as love despises all earthly greatness, it cannot possibly provoke her envy. "She envies
not because, as she desires nothing in this world, she
cannot envy earthly prosperity."1

Hence we must distinguish two kinds of envy, one
evil and the other holy. The evil kind is that which
envies and repines at the worldly goods possessed by
others on this earth. But holy envy, so far from wish
ing to be like, rather compassionates the great ones of
the world, who live in the midst of honors and earthly
pleasures. She seeks and desires God alone, and has no
other aim besides that of loving him as much as she can;
and therefore she has a pious envy of those who love him
more than she does, for she would, if possible, surpass
the very seraphim in loving him.

This is the sole end which pious souls have in view on

1 "Non aemulatur; quia, per hoc quod in praesenti mundo nihil
appetit, invidere terrenis successibus nescit." *Morals in Job,*
Bk. 10, ch. 8.

[324] earth an end which so charms and ravishes the heart
of God with love, that it causes him to say: *You have*

*wounded My heart, My sister; My spouse, you have wounded My heart with one of your eyes.*1 By "one of your eyes " is meant that one end which the espoused soul has in all her devotions and thoughts, namely, to please Almighty God. Men of the world look on things with many eyes, that is, have several disordered views in their actions; as, for instance, to please others, to become honored, to obtain riches, and if nothing else, at least to please them selves; but the saints have but a single eye, with which they keep in view, in all that they do, the sole pleasure of God; and with David they say: *What have I in heaven, and besides You what do I desire upon earth?*2 What do I wish, O my God, in this world or in the next, save You alone? You are my riches, You are the only Lord of my heart. "Let the rich," said St. Paulinus, "enjoy their riches, let the kings enjoy their kingdoms, You, O Christ, are my treasure and my kingdom!"3

And here we must remark, that we must not only per-form good works, but we must perform them well. In order that our works may be good and perfect, they must be done with the sole end of pleasing God. This was the admirable praise bestowed on Jesus Christ : *He has done all things well.*4 Many actions may in them selves be praiseworthy, but from being performed for some other purpose than for the glory of God, they are often of little or no value in his sight. St. Mary Mag-dalene de Pazzi said, "God rewards our actions by the

1 "Vulnerasti cor meum, soror mea Sponsa, vulnerasti cor meum in uno oculorum tuorum." Song of Songs, 4.9.
2 "Quid enim mihi est in coelo? et a te quid volui super terram? . . . Deus cordis mei, et pars mea, Deus, in aeternum." Ps. 72.25, 26.
3 "Sibi habeant divitias suas divites, sibi regna sua reges; nobis gloria, et possesio, et regnum, Christus est." *Letter to Aprum.*
4 "Bene omnia fecit." Mark 7.37.

[325] weight of pure intention."1 As much as to say, that according as our intention is pure, so does the Lord accept of and reward our actions. But, O God, how difficult it is to find an action done solely for You! I remember a holy old man, a religious, who had labored much in the service of God, and died in the reputation of sanctity; now one day, as he cast a glance back at his past life, he said to me in a tone of sadness and fear, "Woe is me! when I consider all the actions of my past life, I do not find one done entirely for God." Oh, this accursed self-love, that makes us lose all or the greater part of the fruit of our good actions! How many in their most holy employments, as of preaching, hearing confessions, giving missions, labor and exert themselves very much, and gain little or nothing because they do not regard God alone, but worldly honor, or self-interest, or the vanity of making an appearance, or at least their own inclination!

Our Lord has said, *Take heed that you do not your justice before men, to be seen by them; otherwise you shall not have a reward of your Father who is in heaven.*2 He that works for his own gratification already receives his wages: *Amen I say to you, they have received their reward.*3 But a reward, indeed, which dwindles into a little smoke, or the pleasure of a day that quickly vanishes, and confers no benefit on the soul. The Prophet Haggai says that who-ever labors for anything else than to please God, puts his reward in a sack full of holes, which, when he comes to open, he finds entirely empty: *And he that has earned wages, put them into a bag with holes.*4 And hence it

1 *Pucch.* Pt. 1, ch. 58.
2 "Attendite ne justitiam vestram faciatis coram hominibus, ut videamini ab eis; alioquin mercedem non habebitis apud Patrem

vestrum qui in coelis est." Matt. 6.1.
3 "Amen, dico vobis, receperunt mercedem suam." Matt. 6.5.
4 "Et qui mercedes congregavit, misit eas in sacculum pertusum. Hag. 1.6.

[326] is that such persons, in the event of their not gaining the object for which they entered on some undertaking, are thrown into great trouble. This is a sign that they had not in view the glory of God alone. He that undertakes a thing solely for the glory of God, is not troubled at all, though his undertaking may fail of success; for, in truth, by working with a pure intention, he has already gained his object, which was to please Almighty God.

The following are the signs which indicate whether we work solely for God in any spiritual undertaking, **1.** If we are not disturbed at the failure of our plans, because when we see it is not God s will, neither is it any longer our will. **2.** If we rejoice at the good done by others, as heartily as if we ourselves had done it. **3.** If we have no preference for one charge more than for another, but willingly accept that which obedience to Superiors enjoins us. **4.** If after our actions we do not seek the thanks or approbation of others, nor are in any way affected if we be found fault with or scolded, being satisfied with having pleased God. And if when the world applauds us we are not puffed up, but meet the vain glory, which might make, itself felt, with the reply of the venerable John of Avila : "Get away, you come too late, for all has been already given to God."

This is to enter into the joy of the Lord; that is, to enjoy the enjoyment of God, as is promised to his faith ful servants: *Well done, you good and faithful servant; because you have been faithful over a few things, ... enter*

*you into the joy of your Lord.*1 And if it falls to our lot to
do something pleasing to God, what more, asks St. John
Chrysostom, can we desire? "If you are found worthy
to perform something that pleases God, do you seek
other recompense than this?"2 The greatest reward, the

1 "Euge, serve bone et fidelis : quia super pauca fuisti fidelis, super
multa te constituam; intra in gaudium Domini tui." Matt. 25.21.
2 "Si dignus fueris agere aliquid quod Deo placet, aliam, praeter
id, mercedem requiris?" *De Compunct.* Bk. 2.

[327] brightest fortune, that can befall a creature, is to give
pleasure to his Creator.

And this is what Jesus Christ looks for from a soul that
loves him: *Put me, he says, as a seal upon your heart,
as a seal upon your arm.*1 He desires us to place him as
a seal on our heart and on our arm: on our heart, in order
that whatever we intend doing, we may intend solely for
the love of God; on our arm, in order that whatever we
do, all may be done to please God; so that God may be
always the sole end of all our thoughts and of all our
actions. St. Teresa said, that he who would become a
saint must live free from every other desire than that of
pleasing God; and her first daughter, the Venerable
Beatrice of the Incarnation, said, "No sum whatever
could repay the slightest thing done for God."2 And
with reason; for all things done to please God are acts
of love which unite us to God, and obtain for us ever
lasting rewards.

Purity of intention is called the heavenly alchemy by
which iron is turned into gold; that is to say, the most
trivial actions (such as to work, to take one's meals, to
take recreation or repose), when done for God, become

the gold of holy love. Wherefore St. Mary Magdalene
de Pazzi believes for certain that those who do all with a
pure intention, go straight to Paradise, without passing
through purgatory. It is related (in the *Spiritual Treas-
ury*) that it was the custom of a pious hermit, before set
ting about any work, to pause a little, and lift his eyes
to heaven; on being questioned why he did so, he replied, "I am taking my aim." By which he meant, that
as the archer, before shooting his arrow, takes his aim,
that he may not miss the mark, so before each action he
made God his aim, in order that it might be sure of pleas-

1 "Pone me ut signaculum super cor tuum, ut signaculum super
brachium tuum." Song of Songs, 8.6.
2 *Foundations*, ch. 12.

[328] ing him. We should do the same; and even during
the performance of our actions, it is very good for us
from time to time to renew our good intention.

Those who have nothing else in view in their undertakings than the divine will, enjoy that holy liberty of
spirit which belongs to the children of God; and this
enables them to embrace everything that pleases Jesus
Christ, however revolting it may be to their own self-love
or human respect. The love of Jesus Christ establishes
his lovers in a state of total indifference; so that all is
the same to them, be it sweet or bitter; they desire nothing for their own pleasure, but all for the pleasure of
God. With the same feelings of peace, they address
themselves to small and great works; to the pleasant
and the unpleasant: it is enough for them if they please
God.

Many, on the other hand, are willing to serve God, but

it must be in such an employment, in such a place, with such companions, or under such circumstances, or else they either quit the work, or do it with an ill-will. Such persons have not freedom of spirit, but are slaves of self-love; and on that account gain very little merit by what they do; they lead a troubled life, because the yoke of Jesus Christ becomes a burden to them. The true lovers of Jesus Christ care only to do what pleases him; and for the reason that it pleases him, when he wills, and where he wills, and in the manner he wills: and whether he wishes to employ them in a state of life honored by the world, or in a life of obscurity and insignificance. This is what is meant by loving Jesus Christ with a pure love; and in this we ought to exercise ourselves, battling against the craving of our self-love, which would urge us to seek important and honorable functions, and such as suit our inclinations.

We must, moreover, be detached from all exercises, even spiritual ones, when the Lord wishes us to be occu-[329] pied in other works of his good pleasure. One day, Father Alvarez, finding himself overwhelmed with business, was anxious to get rid of it, in order to go and pray, because it seemed to him that during that time he was not with God; but our Lord then said to him: "Though I do not keep you with me, let it suffice you that I make use of you."1 This is a profitable lesson for those who are sometimes disturbed at being obliged, by obedience or by love, to leave their accustomed devotions; let them be assured that such disturbances on like occasions do not come from God, but either from the devil or from self-love. "Give pleasure to God, and die." This is the grand maxim of the saints.

Affections and Prayers

O my Eternal God, I offer You my whole heart; but what
sort of heart, O God, is it that I offer You? A heart, created,
indeed, to love You; but which, instead of loving You, has so
many times rebelled against You. But behold, my Jesus, if
there was a time when my heart rebelled against You, now it is
deeply grieved and penitent for the displeasure it has given
You. Yes, my dear Redeemer, I am sorry for having despised
You; and I am determined to do all to obey You, and to love
You at every cost. Oh, draw me wholly to Your love; do this
for the sake of the love which made You die for me on the
cross. I love You, my Jesus; I love You with all my soul;
I love You more than myself, O true and only lover of my soul;
for I find none but You who have sacrificed their life for me.
I weep to think that I have been so ungrateful to You. Unhappy that I am! I was already lost; but I trust that by Your
grace You have restored me to life. And this shall he my life,
to love You always, my sovereign good. Make me love You,
O infinite love, and I ask You for nothing more!

O Mary my mother, accept of me for your servant, and gain
acceptance for me will. Jesus your Son.

1 *Life*, ch. 2.

CHAPTER 4

LOVE IS NOT SNOBBISH
(Not Blind To Spiritual Things)
(Charitas non agit perperam)

[330] [St. Alphonsus, following the Vulgate version of the Bible, entitles this chapter LOVE DOES NOT DEAL PERVERSELY, and he writes of lukewarmness as a prime example of spiritual perversity.]

He that loves Jesus Christ avoids Lukewarmness, and seeks Perfection; the Means of which are: 1. Desire; 2. Resolution; 3. Mental Prayer; 4. Communion; 5. Prayer.

ST. GREGORY, in his explanation of these words, "deals not perversely," says that love, giving herself up more and more to the love of God, ignores whatever is not right and holy.1 The Apostle had already written to the same effect, when he calls love a bond that unites the most perfect virtues together in the soul. *Have love, which is the bond of perfection.*2 And whereas love delights in perfection, she consequently abhors that lukewarmness with which some persons serve God, to the great risk of losing love, divine grace, their very soul, and their all.

1. Lukewarmness

It must be observed that there are two kinds of tepidity or lukewarmness : the one unavoidable, the other avoidable.

I. From the lukewarmness that is unavoidable, the saints themselves are not exempt; and this comprises all

the failings that are committed by us without full con
sent, but merely from our natural frailty. Such are, for
example, distractions at prayers, interior disquietudes,
useless words, vain curiosity, the wish to appear, tastes

1 "Non agit perperam. Quia (charitas), quae se in solum Dei amorem
dilatat, quidquid a rectitudine discrepat, ignorat." *Moralia*, Bk. 10,
ch. 8.
2 "Charitatem habete, quod est vinculum perfectionis." Col. 3.14.

[331] in eating and drinking, the movements of concupiscence not instantly repressed, and such like. We ought to
avoid these defects as much as we possibly can; but, owing to the weakness of our nature, caused by the infection of sin, it is impossible to avoid them altogether.
We ought, indeed, to detest them after committing them,
because they are displeasing to God; but, as we re
marked in the preceding chapter, we ought to beware of
making them a subject of alarm or disquietude. St.
Francis de Sales writes as follows: "All such thoughts
as create disquietude are not from God, who is the prince
of peace; but they proceed always from the devil, or from
self-love, or from the good opinion which we have of
ourselves." 1 Such thoughts, therefore, as disturb us,
must be straightway rejected, and made no account of.

It was said also by the same saint, with regard to in-
deliberate faults, that as they were involuntarily committed, so are they canceled involuntarily. An act of
sorrow, an act of love, is sufficient to cancel them. The
Venerable Sister Mary Crucified, a Benedictine nun, saw
once a globe of fire, on which a number of straws were
cast, and were all immediately reduced to ashes. She was
given to understand by this figure that one act of divine
love, made with fervor, destroys all the defects that we

may have in our soul. The same effect is produced by the holy Communion; according to what we find in the Council of Trent, where the Eucharist is called "an antidote by which we are freed from daily faults."2 Thus the like faults, though they are indeed faults, do not hinder perfection that is, our advancing toward perfection; because in the present life no one attains perfection before he arrives at the kingdom of the blessed.

II. The tepidity, then, that does hinder perfection is that tepidity which is avoidable when a person commits

1 *Letter* 51.
2 "Antidotum, quo liberemur a culpis quotidianis."

[332] deliberate venial faults; because all these faults committed with open eyes can effectually be avoided by the divine grace, even in the present life. Wherefore St. Teresa said: "May God deliver you from deliberate sin, however small it may be."1 Such, for example, are wilful untruths, little detractions, imprecations, expressions of anger, derisions of one's neighbor, cutting words, speeches of self-esteem, animosities nourished in the heart, disordered attachments to persons of a different sex. "These are a sort of worm" (wrote the same saint) " which is not detected before it has eaten into the virtues."2 Hence, in another place, the saint gave this admonition: "By means of small things the devil goes about making holes for great things to enter."3

We should therefore tremble at such deliberate faults; since they cause God to close his hands from bestowing upon us his clearer lights and stronger helps, and they deprive us of spiritual sweetnesses; and the result of them is to make the soul perform all spiritual exercises with great weariness and pain; and so, in course of time, she begins to leave off prayer, Communions, visits to the Blessed Sacrament, and novenas; and, therefore, she will probably leave off all, as has not unfrequently been the case with many unhappy souls.

This is the meaning of that threat which our Lord makes to the tepid: *You are neither cold nor hot; I wish you were cold or hot: but because you are lukewarm . . . I will begin to vomit you out of My mouth.*4 How wonderful! He says, I wish you were cold! What! and is it better to be cold, that is, deprived of grace, than to be tepid?

1 *Way of Perfection*, ch. 42.
2 *Interior Castle*, ch. 3.
3 *Foundations*, ch. 29.
4 "Neque frigidus es, neque calidus; utinam frigidus esses, aut calidus! sed, quia tepidus es, . . . incipiam te evomere." Apoc. (Rev.) 3.15, 16.

[333] Yes, in a certain sense it is better to be cold; because a person who is cold may more easily change his life, being stung by the reproaches of conscience; whereas a tepid person contracts the habit of slumbering on in his faults, without bestowing a thought, or taking any trouble to correct himself; and thus he makes his cure, as it were, desperate. St. Gregory says, "Tepidity, which has cooled down from fervor, is a hopeless state."1 The Ven. Father Louis da Ponte said that he had committed many defects in the course of his life; but that he never had made a truce with his faults. Some there are who shake hands with their faults, and from that springs their ruin; especially when the fault is accompanied with some passionate attachment of self-esteem, of ambition, of liking to be seen, of heaping up money, of resentment

against a neighbor, or of immoderate affection for a per
son of different sex. In such cases there is great danger
of those hairs, as it were, becoming chains, as St. Francis
of Assisi said, which will drag down the soul to hell. At
all events, such a soul will never become a saint, and will
forfeit that beautiful crown, which God had prepared
for her, had she faithfully corresponded to grace. The
bird no sooner feels itself loosed from the snare than it
immediately flies; the soul, as soon as she is loosed from
earthly attachments, immediately flies to God; but while
she is bound, though it be but by the slightest thread, it
is enough to prevent her from flying to God. Oh, how
many spiritual persons there are who do not become
saints, because they will not do themselves the violence
to break away from certain little attachments!

All the evil arises from the little love they have for
Jesus Christ. Those who are puffed up with self-esteem;
those who frequently take to heart occurrences that fall
out contrary to their wishes; who practice great indul-

1 "Tepor (quia fervore defecit) in desperatione est." *On Pastors*,
Pt. 3, 35.

[334] gence towards themselves on account of their health;
who keep their heart open to external objects, and
the mind always distracted, with an eagerness to listen
to, and to know, so many things that have nothing to do
with the service of God, but merely serve to gratify private curiosity; who are ready to resent every little inat-
tention from others, and consequently are often troubled,
and grow remiss in prayer and recollection. One moment
they are all devotion and joy, the next all impatience
and melancholy, just as things happen, according to or
against their humor; all such persons do not love Jesus

Christ, or love him very little, and cast discredit on true devotion.

But suppose any one should find himself sunk in this unhappy state of tepidity, what has he to do? Certainly it is a hard thing for a soul grown lukewarm to resume her ancient fervor; but our Lord has said, that what man cannot do, God can very well do. *The things that are impossible with man, are possible with God.*1 Who ever prays and employs the means is sure to accomplish his desire.

2. Remedies against Lukewarmness

The means to cast off tepidity, and to tread in the path of perfection, are five in number: 1. The desire of perfection; 2. The resolution to attain it; 3. Mental prayer; 4. Frequent Holy Communion; 5. Prayer.

1. Desire of Perfection

The first means, then, is the desire of perfection. Pious desires are the wings which lift us up from earth; for, as St. Laurence Justinian says, desire "supplies strength,

1 "Quae impossibilia sunt apud homines, possibilia sunt apud Deum." Luke 18.27.

[335] and renders pain more light:"1 on the one hand it gives strength to walk towards perfection, and on the other hand it lightens the fatigue of the journey. He who has a real desire of perfection fails not to advance continually towards it; and so advancing, he must finally arrive at it. On the contrary, he who has not the desire of perfection will always go backwards, and always find him

self more imperfect than before. St. Augustine says, that "not to go forward in the way of God is to go backward."2 He that makes no efforts to advance will find himself carried backward by the current of his corrupt nature.

They, then, who say "God does not wish us all to be saints" make a great mistake. Yes, for St. Paul says, *This is the Will of God, your sanctification.*3 God wishes all to be saints, and each one according to his state of life: the religious as a religious; the secular as a secular; the priest as a priest; the married as married; the man of business as a man of business; the soldier as a soldier; and so of every other state of life.

Most beautiful, indeed, are the instructions which my great patroness St. Teresa gives on this subject. She says, in one place, "Let us enlarge our thoughts; for from this we shall derive immense good." Elsewhere she says: "We must beware of having poor desires; but rather put our confidence in God, in order that, by forcing ourselves continually onwards, we may by degrees arrive where, by the divine grace, so many saints have arrived."4 And in confirmation of this she quoted her own experience, having known how courageous souls make considerable progress in a short period of time.

1 "Vires subministrat, poenam exhibet leviorem."
2 "Non progredi, jam reverti est." *Letter* 17,
3 "Haec est voluntas Dei, sanctificatio vestra." 1 Thess. 4.3.
4 *Life*, ch. 13.

[336] "Because," said she, "the Lord takes as much delight in our desires, as if they were put into execution." In another place she says: "Almighty God does not confer

extraordinary favors, except where his love has been earnestly sought after."1 Again, in another passage, she remarks: "God does not fail to repay every good desire even in this life,2 for he is the friend of generous souls, provided only they do not trust in themselves."3 This saint herself was endowed with just such a spirit of generosity; so that she once even said to our Lord, that were she to behold others in paradise enjoying him more than herself, she should not care; but were she to behold any one loving him more than she should love him, this she declared she knew not how she could endure.4

We must, therefore, have a great courage: *The Lord is good to the soul that seeks him.*5 God is surpassingly good and liberal towards a soul that heartily seeks him. Neither can past sins prove a hindrance to our becoming saints, if we only have the sincere desire to become so. St. Teresa remarks: "The devil strives to make us think it pride to entertain lofty desires, and to wish to imitate the saints; but it is of great service to encourage ourselves with the desire of great things, because, although the soul has not all at once the necessary strength, yet she nevertheless makes a bold fight, and rapidly advances."6

The Apostle writes: *To them that love God, all things work together unto good.*7 And the gloss or ancient commentary adds "even sins;" 8 even past sins can contribute

1 *Way of Perfection*, ch. 35.
2 *Life*, ch. 4.
3 *Life*, ch. 13.
4 *Rib.*, Bk. 4. ch. 10.
5 "Bonus est Dominus . . . animoe quaerenti illum." Lam. 3.25.
6 *Life*, ch. 13.
7 "Diligentibus Deum omnia cooperantur in bonum." Rom. 8.28.

8 "Etiam peccata."

[337] to our sanctification, inasmuch as the recollection of them keeps us more humble, and more grateful,
when we witness the favors which God lavishes upon us,
after all our outrages against him. I am capable of
nothing (the sinner should say), nor do I deserve any
thing; I deserve nothing but hell; but I have to deal
with a God of infinite bounty, who has promised to listen
to all that pray to him. Now, as he has rescued me from
a state of damnation, and wishes me to become holy, and
now proffers me his help, I can certainly become a saint,
not by my own strength, but by the grace of my God,
who strengthens me : *I can do all things in Him that
strengthens me.*1 When, therefore, we have once good
desires, we must take courage, and trusting in God, endeavor to put them in execution; but if afterwards we
encounter any obstacle in our spiritual enterprises, let us
repose quietly on the will of God. God's will must be
preferred before every good desire of our own. St. Mary
Magdalene de Pazzi would sooner have remained void of
all perfection than possess it without the will of God.

2. *Resolution*

The second means of perfection is the resolution to
belong wholly to God. Many are called to perfection;
they are urged on towards it by grace, they conceive, a
desire of it; but because they never really resolve to
acquire it, they live and die in the ill-odor of their tepid
and imperfect life. The desire of perfection is not
enough, if it be not followed up by a stern resolve to
attain it. How many souls feed themselves on desires
alone, but never make withal one step in the way of God!
It is of such desires that the wise man speaks when

he says : *Desires kill the slothful.*2 The slothful man is
ever desiring, but never resolves to take the means suit-

1 "Omnia possum in eo qui me confortat." Phil. 4.13.
2 "Desideria occidunt pigrum." Prov. 21.25.

[338] able to his state of life to become a saint. He says:
"Oh, if I were but in solitude, and not in this house!
 Oh, if I could but go and reside in another monastery,
I would give myself entirely up to God!" And meanwhile he cannot support a certain companion; he cannot
put up with a word of contradiction; he is dissipated
about many useless cares; he commits a thousand faults
of gluttony, of curiosity, and of pride; and yet he sighs
out to the wind: "Oh, if I had only...!" or "Oh, if I could
only...!" etch. Such desires do more harm than good; because some regale themselves upon them, and in the
meantime go on leading a life of imperfection. It was a
saying of St. Francis de Sales: "I do not approve of a
person who, being engaged in some duty or vocation,
stops to sigh for some other kind of life that is incompati-
ble with his actual position, or for other exercises un-
fitted for his present state; for it merely serves to dissi-
pate his heart, and makes him languish in his necessary
duties."1

We must, therefore, desire perfection, and resolutely
take the means towards it. St. Teresa says: "God only
looks for one resolution on our part, and will afterwards
do all the rest himself: 2 the devil has no fear of irresolute
souls."3 For this reason mental prayer must be used,
in order to take the means which lead to perfection. Some
make much prayer, but never come to a practical conclusion. The same saint said: "I would rather have a
short prayer, which produces great fruits, than a prayer

of many years, wherein a soul never gets further than resolving to do something worthy of Almighty God."4 And elsewhere she says: "I have learned by experience that whoever, at the beginning, brings himself to the resolution of doing some great work, however difficult it

1 *Introduction to the Devout Life*, ch. 37.
2 *Foundations*, ch. 28.
3 *Way of Perfection*, ch. 24.
4 *Life*, ch. 39.

[339] may be, if he does so to please God, he has no reason to be afraid."

The first resolution must be to make every effort, and to die rather than commit any deliberate sin whatever, however small it may be. It is true that all our endeavors, without the divine assistance, cannot enable us to vanquish temptations; but God wishes us on our part frequently to use this violence with ourselves, because then he will afterwards supply us with his grace, will help our weakness, and enable us to gain the victory. This resolution removes from us every obstacle to our going forward, and at the same time gives us great courage, because it affords us an assurance of being in the grace of God. St. Francis de Sales writes: "The best security we can possess in this world of being in the grace of God, consists not indeed in feeling that we have his love, but in a pure and irrevocable abandonment of our entire being into his hands, and in the firm resolution of never consenting to any sin, either great or small."1 This is what is meant by being of a delicate conscience. Be it observed, that it is one thing to be of a delicate con science, and another to be of a scrupulous conscience. To be of a delicate conscience is requisite to become a saint; but to be scrupulous is a defect, and does harm; and on this account we must obey our directors, and rise above scruples, which are nothing else but vain and unreasonable alarms.

Hence it is necessary to resolve on choosing the best, not only what is agreeable to God, but what is most agreeable to him, without any reserve. St. Francis de Sales says: "We must start with a strong and constant resolution to give ourselves wholly to God, and protest to him that for the future we wish to be his without any Deserve, and then we must afterwards often renew this

1 *Spirit of St Francis de Sales*, ch. 9.

[340] same resolution."1 St. Andrew Avellini made a vow to advance daily in perfection. It is not necessary for every one who wishes to become a saint to make it the matter of a vow; but he must endeavor every day to make some steps forward in perfection. St. Laurence Justinian has written: "When a person is really making way, he feels in himself a continual desire of advancing; and the more he improves in perfection, the more this desire increases; because as his interior light increases each day more and more, he seems to himself always to be wanting in every virtue, and to be doing no good at all; and if, per chance, he is aware of some good he does, it always ap pears to him very imperfect, and he makes small account of it. The consequence is, he is continually laboring to acquire perfection without ever feeling wearied."

And we must begin quickly, and not wait for tomorrow. Who knows whether we shall afterwards find time or not! Ecclesiastes counsels us: *Whatsoever your hand is able to do, do it earnestly.*2 What you can do, do it quickly, and defer it not; and he adduces the reason why: *For neither work, nor reason, nor wisdom, nor knowledge shall be in hell, to where you are hastening.*3 Because in the next life there is no more time to work, nor free will to merit, nor prudence to do well, nor wisdom or experience to take good counsel by, for after death what is done is done.

A nun of the convent of Torre de Specchi in Rome, whose name was Sister Bonaventura, led a very lukewarm sort of life. There came a religious, Father Lancicius, to give the spiritual exercises to the nuns, and Sister Bonaventura, feeling no inclination to shake off

1 *Love of God*, Bk. 12, ch. 8.
2 "Quodcumque facere potest manus tua, instanter operate. " Eccles. 9.10.
3 "Quia nec opus, nec ratio, nec sapientia nec scientia, erunt apud inferos, quo tu properas." *Ibid.*

[341] her tepidity, began to listen to the exercises with no good will. But at the very first sermon she was won by divine grace, so that she immediately went to the feet of the Father who preached, and said to him, with a tone of real determination, "Father, I wish to become a saint, and quickly a saint." And, by the assistance of God, she did so; for she lived only eight months after that event, and during that short time she lived and died a saint.

David said: *And I said, now have I begun.*1 So likewise exclaimed St. Charles Borromeo: "Today I begin to serve God." And we should act in the same way as if we had hitherto done no good whatever; for, indeed, all that we do for God is nothing, since we are bound to do it. Let us therefore each day resolve to begin afresh to belong wholly to God. Neither let us stop to observe what or how others do. They who become truly saints are few. St. Bernard says: "One cannot be perfect with out being singular."2 If we would imitate the common run of men, we should always remain imperfect, as for the most part they are. We must overcome all, renounce all, in order to gain all. St. Teresa said: "Because we do not come to the conclusion cf giving all our affection to God, so neither does he give all his love to us."3 Oh, God, how little is all that is given to Jesus Christ, who has given his blood and his life for us! "However much we give," says the same saint, "is but dirt, in compari- son of one single drop of blood shed for us by our Blessed Lord."4 The saints know not how to spare themselves, when there is a question of pleasing a God who gave himself wholly, without reserve, on purpose to oblige us to deny him nothing. St. John Chrysostom

1 "Et dixi: Nunc coepi." Ps. 76.11.
2 "Perfectum esse non potest nisi singulare."
3 *Life*, ch. 2.
4 *Life*, ch 39.

[342] wrote: "He gave all to you, and kept nothing for him self." 1 God has bestowed his entire self upon you; there is, then, no excuse for you to behave reservedly with God. He has even died for us all, says the Apostle, in order that each one of us may live only for him who died for us: *Christ died for all; that they also who live may not now live to themselves, but unto Him who died for them.*2

3. Mental Prayer

The third means of becoming a saint is mental prayer.

John Gerson writes: 3 "That he who does not meditate on the eternal truths cannot, without a miracle, lead the Life of a Christian. The reason is, because without mental prayer light fails us, and we walk in the dark. The truths of faith are not seen by the eyes of the body, but by the eyes of the mind, when we meditate; he that fails to meditate on them, fails to see them, and therefore walks in the dark; and being in the dark, he easily grows attached to sensible things, for the sake of which he then comes to despise the eternal." St. Teresa wrote as follows to the Bishop of Osma: "Although we seem to discover in our selves no imperfections; yet, when God opens the eyes of the soul, which he will often do in prayer, then they plainly appear."4 And St. Bernard had before said, that he who does not meditate "does not abhor himself, merely be cause he does not know himself."5 "Prayer," says the saint, "regulates the affections, directs the actions,"6 keeps the affections of the soul in order, and directs all our actions to God; but without prayer the affections

1 "Totum tibi dedit, nihil sibi reliquit."
2 "Pro omnibus mortuus est Christus, ut et qui vivunt, jam non sibi vivant, sed ei qui pro ipsis mortuus est." 2 Cor. 5.15.
3 *De Med. cons.* 7.
4 *Letter* 8.
5 "Seipsum non exhorret, quia nee sentit." *On Consideration*, Bk. 1, ch. 2.
6 "Consideratio regit affectus, dirigit actus." *Ibid.* ch. 7.

[343] become attached to the earth, the actions conform themselves to the affections, and in this manner all runs into disorder.

We read of an awful example of this in the life of the Venerable Sister Mary Crucified of Sicily. While this servant of God was praying, she heard a devil making a boast that he had succeeded in withdrawing a religious from the community-prayer; and she saw in spirit, that after this omission the devil tempted her to consent to a grievous sin, and that she was on the point of yielding. She immediately accosted her, and by a timely admonition prevented her from falling. Abbe Diodes said, that whoever leaves off prayer "very shortly becomes either a beast or a devil."1

He therefore that leaves off prayer will leave off loving Jesus Christ. Prayer is the blessed furnace in which the fire of holy love is enkindled and kept alive: And in my meditation a fire shall flame out.2 It was said by St. Catherine of Bologna: "The person that forgoes the practice of prayer cuts that string which binds the soul to God." It follows that the devil, finding the soul cold in divine love, will have little difficulty in inducing her to partake of some poisonous fruit or other. St. Teresa said, on the contrary, "Whosoever perseveres in prayer, let him hold for a certainty, that with however many sins the devil may surround him, the Lord will eventually bring him into the haven of salvation."3 In another place she says, "Whoever halts not in the way of prayer arrives sooner or later."4 And elsewhere she writes, "that it is on this account that the devil labors so hard to withdraw souls from prayer, because he well knows that he has missed gaining those who faithfully perse-

1 *Pall. Hist. laus.* ch. 98.
2 "In meditatione mea exardescet ignis." Ps. 38.4.
3 *Life*, ch. 8.
4 *Life*, ch. 19.

[344] vere in prayer." Oh, how great are the benefits that, flow from prayer! In prayer we conceive holy thoughts, we

practice devout affections, we excite great desires, and form efficacious resolutions to give ourselves wholly to God; and thus the soul is led for his sake to sacrifice earthly pleasures and all disorderly appetites. It was said by St. Aloysius Gonzaga: "There will never be much perfection without much prayer." Let him who longs for perfection mark well this notable saying of the saint.

We should not go to prayer in order to taste the sweetness of divine love; whoever prays from such a motive will lose his time, or at least derive little advantage from it. A person should begin to pray solely to please God, that is, solely to learn what the will of God is in his regard, and to beg of him the help to put it in practice. The Venerable Father Antony Torres said: "To carry the cross without consolation makes souls fly to perfection. Prayer unattended with sensible consolations confers greater fruit on the soul. But pitiable is the poor soul that leaves off prayer, because she finds no relish in it." St. Teresa said: "When a soul leaves off prayer, it is as if she cast herself into hell without any need of devils."1

It results, too, from the practice of prayer, that a person constantly thinks of God. "The true lover" (says St. Teresa) "is ever mindful of the beloved one. And hence it follows that persons of prayer are always speaking of God, knowing, as they do, how pleasing it is to God that his lovers should delight in conversing about him, and on the love he bears them, and that thus they should endeavor to enkindle it in others."2 The same saint wrote: "Jesus Christ is always found present at the conversations of the servants of God, and he is very much gratified to be the subject of their delight."3

1 *Life*, ch. 19.
2 *Foundations*, ch. 5.
3 *Life*, ch. 34.

[345] Prayer, again, creates that desire of retiring into
solitude, in order to converse alone with God, and to main-
tain interior recollection in the discharge of necessary
external duties; I say necessary, such as the management
of one's family, or of the performance of duties required
of us by obedience; because a person of prayer must
love solitude, and avoid dissipation in superfluous and
useless affairs, otherwise he will lose the spirit of recollection, which is a great means of preserving union with
God: *My sister, my spouse is a garden enclosed.*1 The soul
espoused to Jesus Christ must be a garden closed against
all creatures, and must not admit into her heart other
thoughts, nor other business, but those of God or for
God. Hearts thrown open never become saints. The
saints, who have to labor in gaining souls to God, do not
lose their recollection in the midst of all their labors,
either of preaching, confessing, reconciling enemies, or
assisting the sick. The same rule holds good with those
who have to apply to study. How many from excessive
study, and a desire to become learned, become neither
holy nor learned, because true learning consists in the
science of the saints; that is to say, in knowing how to
love Jesus Christ; whereas, on the contrary, divine love
brings with it knowledge and every good: *All good things
came to me together with Her*,2 that is, with holy love.
The Venerable John Berchmans had an extraordinary
love for study, but by his great virtue he never allowed
study to interfere with his spiritual interests. The Apostle
exhorts us: *Not to be more wise than it behoves to be
wise, but to be wise unto sobriety.*3 A priest especially
must have knowledge; he must know things, because he

1 "Hortus conclusus, soror mea sponsa." Song of Songs, 4.12.
2 "Venerunt autem mihi omnia bona pariter cum illa." Wisd. 7.11.
3 "Non plus sapere, quam oportet sapere, sed sapere ad sobrietatem."
Rom. 12.3.

[346] has to instruct others in the divine law: *For the lips of the priest shall keep knowledge, and they shall seek the law at his mouth.*1 He must have knowledge, but unto sobriety. He that leaves prayer for study shows that in his study he seeks himself, and not God. He that seeks God leaves study (if it be not absolutely necessary), in order not to omit prayer.

Besides, the greatest evil is, that without mental prayer we do not pray at all. I have spoken frequently in my spiritual works of the necessity of prayer, and more especially in a little volume entitled, *On Prayer, the great Means*, etch.; and in the present chapter also I will briefly say a few other things. It will be sufficient then to quote here the opinion of the Venerable Palafox, Bishop of Osma, in his remarks on the letters of St. Teresa: "How can love last, unless God grant us perseverance? How will the Lord grant us perseverance unless we ask it of him? And how shall we ask it of him except by prayer? Without prayer there is no communication with God for the preservation of virtue."2 And so it is, because he that neglects mental prayer sees very little into the wants of his soul, he knows little of the dangers of his salvation, of the means to be used in order to overcome temptations; and so, understanding little of the necessity of prayer, he leaves off praying, and will certainly be lost.

Then as regards subjects for meditation, nothing is more useful than to meditate on the *Four Last Things* - death, judgment, hell, and heaven; but it is of especial advantage to meditate on death, and to imagine ourselves expiring on the bed of sickness, with the crucifix in our hands, and on the point of entering into eternity. But above all, to one that loves Jesus Christ, and is

1 "Labia enim sacerdotis custodient scientiam, et legem requirent ex ore ejus." Mal. 2.7.
2 *Letter* 8.

[347] anxious always to increase in his love, no consideration is more efficacious than that of the Passion of the Redeemer. St. Francis de Sales calls "Mount Calvary the mountain of lovers." All the lovers of Jesus Christ love to abide on this mountain, where no air is breathed but the air of divine love. When we see a God dying for our love, and dying in order to gain our love (*He loved us, and delivered Himself up for us* 1), it is impossible not to love him ardently. Such darts of love continually issue forth from the wounds of Christ crucified as pierce even hearts of stone. Oh, happy is he who is ever going during this life to the heights of Calvary! O blessed Mount! O lovely Mount! O beloved Mount! and who shall ever leave you more! A Mount that sends forth flames to enkindle the souls that perseveringly abide upon you!

4. *Frequent Communion*

The fourth means of perfection, and even of perseverance in the grace of God, is frequently to receive the Holy Communion, of which we have already spoken in the Introduction, II., page 275, where we affirmed that a soul can do nothing more pleasing to Jesus Christ than to receive him often in the Sacrament of the Altar. St. Teresa said : "There is no better help to perfection than frequent Communion : oh, how admirably does the Lord bring such a soul to perfection!" And she adds, that, ordinarily speaking, they who communicate most frequently are found further advanced in perfection; and that there is greater spirituality in those communities where frequent Communion is the custom. For this reason it is that, as we find declared in a decree of Innocent XI., in 1679, the holy Fathers have so highly extolled, and so much promoted, the practice of frequent and even of daily Communion. Holy Communion, as the Council

1 "Dilexit nos et tradidit semetipsum pro nobis." Eph. 5.2.

[348] of Trent tells us, delivers us from daily faults, and preserves us from mortal ones. St. Bernard asserts 1 that Communion represses the movements of anger and incontinence, which are the two passions that most frequently and most violently assail us. St. Thomas says,2 that Communion defeats the suggestions of the devil. And finally, St. John Chrysostom says that Communion pours into our souls a great inclination to virtue, and a promptitude to practice it; and at the same time imparts to us a great peace, by which the path of perfection is made very sweet and easy to us. Besides, there is no sacrament so capable of kindling the divine love in souls as the Holy Sacrament of the Eucharist, in which Jesus Christ bestows on us his whole self, in order to unite us all to himself by means of holy love. Wherefore the Venerable Father John of Avila said : "Whoever deters souls from frequent Communion does the work of the devil." Yes; for the devil has a great horror of this sacrament, from which souls derive immense strength to advance in divine love.

But the proper preparation is requisite to communicate well The first preparation, or, in other terms, the remote preparation, to be able to go to Communion daily, or several times in the week, is: **1.** To keep free from all deliberate affection to sin that is, to sin committed, as we say, with the eyes open. **2.** The practice of much mental prayer. **3.** The mortification of the senses and of the passions. St. Francis de Sales 3 teaches as follows: "Whoever has overcome the greatest part of his bad inclinations, and has arrived at a notable degree of perfection, can communicate every day." The angelic Doctor St. Thomas says, 4 that any one who knows by experience that his soul derives an increase of divine love from the Holy Communion may communicate

1 *In Coena Domini*, sermon 1.
2 *S. Theol.* 3, q. 79. a. 6.
3 *Introduction to the Devout Life*, ch. 20.
4 *In 4 Sent.* d. 12, q. 3, a. 1, s. 2.

[349] daily. Hence Innocent XI, in the above-mentioned decree, said that the greater or less frequency of Holy Communion must rest on the decision of the confessor who ought to be guided in this matter by the profit which he sees accrue to the souls under his direction. In the next place, the proximate preparation for Communion is that which is made on the morning itself of Communion, for which there is need of at least half an hour of mental prayer.

To reap also more abundant fruit from Communion, we must make a long thanksgiving. Father John of Avila said that the time after communion is "a time to gain treasures of graces." St. Mary Magdalene de Pazzi used to say that no time can be more calculated to in flame us with divine love than the time immediately after our Communion. And St. Teresa says: "After Communion let us be careful not to lose so good an opportunity of negotiating with God. His divine majesty is not accustomed to pay badly for his lodging, if he meets with a good reception."1

There are certain pusillanimous souls, who, on being exhorted to communicate more frequently, reply: "But I am not worthy." But, do you not know, that the more you refrain from Communion, the more unworthy you become of it? Because, deprived of Holy Communion, you will have less strength, and will commit many faults. Well, then, obey your director, and be guided by him : faults do not forbid Holy Communion, when they are not committed with full will; besides, among your failings, the greatest is, not to submit to what your spiritual Father says to you.

"But in my past life I was very bad." And I reply, that you must know, that he who is weakest has most need of the physician and of medicine. Jesus in the Blessed Sacrament is our physician and medicine as well.

1 *Way of Perfection*, ch. 35.

[350] St. Ambrose said : "I, who am always sinning, have always need of medicine."1 You will then say, perhaps-: "But my confessor does not tell me to communicate oftener." If, then, he does not tell you to do so, ask his permission to communicate oftener. Should he deny you, obey him; but in the mean time make him the request. "It would seem pride." It would be pride if you were to wish to communicate against his will, but not when you ask his consent with humility. This

heavenly bread requires hunger. Jesus loves to be desired, says a devout author; "He thirsts to be thirsted for."2 And what a thought is this: "Today I have communicated, and to-morrow I have to communicate." Oh, how such a reflection keeps the soul attentive to avoid all defects and to do the will of God! "But I have no devotion." If you mean sensible devotion, it is not necessary, neither does God always grant it even to his most beloved souls. It is enough for you to have the devotion of a will determined to belong wholly to God, and to make progress in his divine love. John Gerson says, 3 that he who abstains from Communion because he does not feel that devotion which he would like to feel, acts like a man who does not approach the fire because he does not feel warm.

Alas, my God, how many souls, from not applying themselves to lead a life of greater recollection and more detachment from earthly things, care not to seek Holy Communion! and this is the true cause of their not wishing to communicate more frequently. They are well aware that to be wishing always to appear, to dress with vanity, to be fond of nice eating and drinking, of bodily comforts, of conversations and amusements, does not

1 "Qui semper pecco, semper debeo habere medicum."
De Sacram. Bk. 4, ch. 6.
2 "Sitit sitiri Deus." *Tetr. Sent.* 37.
3 *Sup. Magn.* tr. 9, p. 3.

[351] harmonize with frequent Communion; they know that more prayer is required, more mortification, as well internal as external, more seclusion; and on this account they are ashamed to approach the altar more frequently. Without doubt, such souls are right to refrain from fre-

quent Communion as long as they find themselves in that unhappy state of lukewarmness; but whoever is called to a more perfect life should lay aside this lukewarmness, if he would not greatly risk his eternal salvation.

It will be found likewise to contribute very much to keep fervor alive in the soul, often to make a spiritual Communion, so much recommended by the Council of Trent, 1 which exhorts all the faithful to practice it. The spiritual Communion, as St. Thomas says,2 consists in an ardent desire to receive Jesus Christ in the Holy Sacrament; and therefore the saints were careful to make it several times in the day. The method of making it is this: "My Jesus, I believe that You are really present in the Most Holy Sacrament. I love You, and I desire You; come to my soul. I embrace You; and I beseech You never to allow me to be separated from You again." Or more briefly thus: "My Jesus, come to me; I desire You; I embrace You; let us remain ever united together." This spiritual Communion maybe practiced several times a day: when we make our prayer, when we make our visit to the Blessed Sacrament, and especially when we attend Mass at the moment of the priest's Communion. The Dominican Sister Blessed Angela of the Cross said: "If my confessor had not taught me this method of communicating spiritually several times a day, I should not have trusted myself to live."

5. *Prayer*

The fifth and most necessary means for the spiritual

1 Session 13. ch. 8,
2 *S. Theol.* Pt. 3. q. 79, a. 1.

[352] life, and for obtaining the love of Jesus Christ, is prayer. In the first place, I say that by this means God convinces us of the great love he bears us. What greater proof of affection can a person give to a friend than to say to him, "My friend, ask anything you like of me, and I will give it you"? Now, this is precisely what our Lord says to us: *Ask, and it shall be given you; seek, and you shall find.*1 Wherefore prayer is called all-powerful with God to obtain every blessing: "Prayer, though it is one, can effect all things," as Theodoret says;2 whoever prays, obtains from God whatever he chooses. The words of David are beautiful : *Blessed be God who has not turned away my prayer, nor his mercy from me.*3 Commenting on this passage, St. Augustine says, "As long as you see yourself not failing in prayer, be assured that the divine mercy will not fail you either." And St. John Chrysostom: "We always obtain, even while we are still praying."4 When we pray to God he grants us the grace we ask for, even before we have ended our petition. If then we are poor, let us blame only ourselves, since we are poor merely because we wish to be poor, and so we are undeserving of pity. What sympathy can there be for a beggar, who, having a very rich master, and one most desirous to provide him with everything if he will only ask for it, nevertheless chooses still to continue in his poverty sooner than ask for what he wants. "Behold," says the Apostle, "our God is ready to enrich all who call upon him": *Rich unto all that call upon Him.*5

Humble prayer, then, obtains all from God; but we

1 "Petite, et dabitur vobis; quaerite, et invenietis." Matt. 7.7.
2 "Oratio cum sit una omnia potest." *Ap. Rodr.* Pt. 1, tr. 5, ch. 14; Wisd. 7.27.

3 "Benedictus Deus, qui non amovit orationem meam et misericordiam suam a me." Ps. 65.20.
4 "Semper obtinemus, etiam dum adhuc oramus."
5 "Dives in omnibus qui invocant illum." Rom. 10.12.

[353] must be persuaded at the same time, that if it be
useful, it is no less necessary for our salvation. It is certain
that we absolutely require the divine assistance, in order
to overcome temptations; and sometimes, in certain
more violent assaults, the sufficient grace which God
gives to all, might possibly enable us to resist them; but
on account of our inclination to evil, it will not ordinarily be sufficient, and we shall stand in need of a special
grace. Whoever prays obtains this grace; but whoever
prays not, obtains it not, and is lost. And this is more
especially the case with regard to the grace of final perseverance, of dying in the grace of God, which is the grace
absolutely necessary for our salvation, and without
which we should be lost forever. St. Augustine 1 says
of this grace, that God only bestows it on those who
pray. And this is the reason why so few are saved, be
cause few indeed are mindful to beg of God this grace
of perseverance.

Therefore the holy Fathers say, that prayer is necessary
for us, not merely as a necessity of precept (so that theologians say, that he who neglects for a month to recommend
to God the affair of his salvation is not exempt from mortal
sin), but also as a necessity of means, which is as much as
to say, that whoever does not pray cannot possibly be
saved. And the reason of it is, in short, because we can
not obtain eternal salvation without the help of divine
grace, and this grace Almighty God only accords to
those who pray. And because temptations, and the
dangers of falling into God's displeasure, continually be

set us, so ought our prayers to be continual. Hence St. Thomas declares that continual prayer is necessary for a man to save himself: "Unceasing prayer is necessary to man, that he may enter heaven."2 And Jesus Christ

1 *De Dono perseverantia.* ch. 16.
2 "Necessaria est homini jugis oratio, ad hoc quod coelum introeat." *S. Theol.* Pt. 3, q. 39, a. 5.

[354] himself had already said the same thing: *We ought always to pray, and not to faint.*1 And afterwards the Apostle: *Pray without ceasing.*2 During the interval in which we shall cease to pray, the devil will conquer us. And though the grace of perseverance can in no wise be merited by us, as the Council of Trent teaches us,3 nevertheless St. Augustine says, "that in a certain sense we can merit it by prayer."4 The Lord wishes to dispense his grace to us, but he will be entreated first; even more, as St. Gregory remarks, he wills to be importuned, and in a manner constrained by our prayers: "God wishes to be prayed to, he wishes to be compelled, he wishes to be, as it were, vanquished by our importunity."5 St. Mary Magdalene de Pazzi said, "that when we ask graces of God, he not only hears us, but in a certain sense thanks us." Yes, because God, as the infinite goodness, in wishing to pour out himself upon others, has, so to speak, an infinite longing to distribute his gifts; but he wishes to be besought: hence it follows, that when he sees himself entreated by a soul, he receives so much pleasure, that in a certain sense he thanks that soul for it.

Well, then, if we wish to preserve ourselves in the grace of God till death, we must act the mendicant, and keep our mouths open to beg for God's help, always repeating, "My Jesus, mercy; never let me be separated from You; O Lord, come to my aid; My God, assist me!" This was the unceasing prayer of the ancient Fathers of the desert: "Incline unto my aid, O God:

1 "Oportet semper orare, et non deficere." Luke 18.1.
2 "Sine intermissione orate." 1 Thess. 5.17.
3 Session. 6, ch. 13.
4 "Hoc Dei donum suppliciter emereri potest." *De Dono pers.* ch. 6.
5 "Vult Deus rogari, vult cogi, vult quadam importunitate vinci. *On the Psalms,* 6.

[355] *O Lord, make haste to help me!*1 O Lord, help me, and help me soon; for if You delay Your assistance, I shall fall and perish!" And this above all must be practiced in the moment of temptation; he who acts otherwise is lost.

And let us have a great faith in prayer. God has promised to hear him that prays: *Ask, and you shall receive.* 2 How can we doubt, says St. Augustine, since God has bound himself by express promise, and cannot fail to grant us the favors we ask of him? "By promising he has made himself our debtor."3 In recommending our selves to God, we must have a sure confidence that God hears us, and then we shall obtain whatever we want. Behold what Jesus Christ says: *All things, whatsoever you ask when ye pray, believe that you shall receive, and they shall come unto you.*4

"But," some one may say, "I am a sinner, and do not deserve to be heard." But Jesus Christ says: *Every one that asks, receives.*5 Every one, be he just, or be he a sinner. St. Thomas teaches us that the efficacy of prayer to obtain graces does not depend on our merits, but on the mercy of God, who has promised to hear every one

who prays to him.6 And our Redeemer, in order to re
move from us all fear when we pray, said: *Amen, amen, I
say to you, if you shall ask the Father anything in My name,
He will give it you.*7 As though he would say: Sinners,

1 "Deus, in adjutorium meum intende; Domine, ad adjuvandum
me festina." Ps. 69.2.
2 "Petite, et accipietis." John 16.24.
3 "Promittendo, debitorem se fecit." Sermon 110.
4 "Omnia quaecumque orantes petitis, credite quia accipietis,
et evenient vobis." Mark 11.24.
5 "Omnis qui petit, accipit." Luke 11.10.
6 "Oratio in impetrando non innititur merito, sed divinae miseri-
cordiae." *S. Theol.* 2-2, q. 178, a. 2.
7 "Amen, amen, dico vobis: si quid petieritis Patrem in nomine
meo, dabit vobis." John 16.23.

[356] you have no merits of your own to obtain graces,
wherefore do in this manner; when you would obtain
graces, ask them of my Father in my name; that is,
through my merits and through my love; and then ask
as many as you choose, and they shall be granted to you.
But let us mark well those words, "In My name;" which
signify (as St. Thomas explains it), "in the name of the
Savior;" or, in other words, that the graces which we
ask must be graces which regard our eternal salvation;
and consequently we must remark that the promise does
not regard temporal favors; these our Lord grants, when
they are profitable for our eternal welfare; if they would
prove otherwise, he refuses them. So that we should
always ask for temporal favors, on condition that they
will benefit our soul. But should they be spiritual
graces, then they require no condition; but with confidence, and a sure confidence, we should say: "Eternal
Father, in the name of Jesus Christ deliver me from this
temptation: grant me holy perseverance, grant me Your

love, grant me heaven." We can likewise ask these
graces of Jesus Christ in his own name; that is, by his
merits, since we have his promise also to this effect: *If
you shall ask Me anything in My name, that I will do.*1

And while we pray to God, let us not forget to recommend ourselves at the same time to Mary, the dispenser
of graces. St. Bernard says that it is Almighty God
who bestows the graces; but he bestows them through
the hands of Mary: "Let us seek grace, and let us seek
it through Mary; because what she seeks she finds, and
cannot be refused."2 If Mary prays for us, we are safe;
for every petition of Mary is heard and she can never
meet with a repulse.

1 "Si quid petieritis me in nomine meo, hoc faciam." John 14.14.
2 "Quaeramus gratiam, et per Mariam quaeramus; quia, quod
quaerit, invenit, et frustrari non potest." *De Aquaeducto.*

Affections and Prayers

[357] O Jesus, my love, I am determined to love You as much
as I can, and I wish to become a saint; and I wish to become a
saint for this reason, in order to give You pleasure, and to
love You exceedingly in this life and the next! I can do nothing
of myself, but You can do all things; and I know that You
wish me to become a saint. I see already that by Your grace
my soul sighs only for You, and seeks nothing else but You.
I wish to live no more for myself; You desire me to be wholly
Your, and I desire to be wholly Your. Come, and unite me to
Yourself, and Yourself to me. You are infinite goodness; You
are he who have loved me so much; You are, indeed, too loving and too lovely; how, then, can I love anything but You?
I prefer Your love before all the things of this world; You are
the sole object, the sole end of all my affections. I leave all to
be occupied solely in loving You, my Redeemer, my Com-

forter, my hope, my love, and my all. I will not despair of be
coming a saint on account of the sins of my past life; for I
know, my Jesus, that You did die in order to pardon the
truly penitent. I love You now with my whole heart, with my
whole soul; I love You more than myself, and I bewail, above
every other evil, ever having had the misfortune to despise You,
my sovereign good. Now 1 am no longer my own, I am Your;

God of my heart, dispose of me as You please. In order to
please You, I accept of all the tribulations You may choose
to send me sickness, sorrow, troubles, disgraces, poverty, persecution, desolation I accept all to please You : in like manner

1 accept of the death You have decreed for me, with all the anguish and crosses which may accompany it: it is enough if
You grant me the grace to love You exceedingly. Lend
me Your assistance; give me strength henceforth to compensate,
by my love, for all the bitterness that I have caused You in
past time, O only love of my soul!

O Queen of Heaven, O Mother of God, O great advocate of
sinners, I trust in you!

CHAPTER 5

LOVE IS NOT PUFFED UP
(Humility)
(*Charitas non inflatur*)

He that loves Jesus Christ is not vain of his own Worth, but humbles himself, and is glad to be humbled by Others

[358] A proud person is like a balloon filled with air, which seems, indeed, great; but whose greatness, in reality, is nothing more than a little air; which, as soon as the balloon is opened, is quickly dispersed. He who loves God is humble, and is not elated at seeing any worth in him self; because he knows that whatever he possesses is the gift of God, and that of his own he has only nothingness and sin; so that this knowledge of the divine favors bestowed on him humbles him the more; while he is conscious of being so unworthy, and yet so favored by God.

St. Teresa says, in speaking of the especial favors she received from God: "God does with me as they do with a house, which, when about to fall, they prop up with supports." When a soul receives a loving visit from God, and feels within herself an unwonted fervor of divine love, accompanied with tears, or with a great tenderness of heart, let her beware of supposing that God so favors her, in reward for some good action; but let her then humble herself the more, concluding that God caresses her in order that she may not forsake him; otherwise, were she to make such favors the subject of vain complacency, imagining herself more privileged, because she receives greater gifts from God than others, such a fault would induce God to deprive her of his favors. Two things are chiefly requisite for the stability of a house the foundation and the roof; the foundation [359] in us must be humility, in acknowledging ourselves good for nothing, and capable of nothing; and the roof is the divine assistance, in which alone we ought to put all our trust.

Whenever we behold ourselves unusually, favored by God, we must humble ourselves the more. When St. Teresa received any special favor, she used to strive to place before her eyes all the faults she had ever committed; and thus the Lord received her into closer union with himself: the more a soul confesses herself undeserving of any favors, the more God enriches her with his graces. Thais, who was first a sinner and then a saint, humbled herself so profoundly before God that she dared not even mention his name; so that she had not the courage to say, "My God;" but she said, "My Creator, have mercy on me!"1 And St. Jerome writes, that in recompense for such humility, she saw a glorious throne prepared for her in heaven. In the life of St. Margaret of Cortona we read the same thing; that, when our Lord visited her one day with greater tokens of tenderness and love, she exclaimed: "But, O Lord, have You then forgotten what I have been? Is it possible that You can repay all my outrages against You with so exquisite sweetness?" And God replied, that when a soul loves him, and cordially repents of having offended him, he forgets all her past infidelities; as, indeed, he formerly spoke by the mouth of Ezekiel: *But if the wicked do penance . . . . I will not remember all his iniquities.*2 And in proof of this, he showed her a high throne, which he had prepared for her in heaven in the midst of the seraphim. Oh, that we could only well comprehend the value of humility! A single act of humility is worth more than all the riches of the universe.

1 "Qui plasmasti me, miserere mei." *Lives of the Fathers,* Bk. 1.
2 "Si autem impius egerit poenitentiam, . . . omnium iniquitatum ejus, quas operatus est, non recordabor." Ezech. 18.21, 22.

[360] It was the saying of St. Teresa, "Think not that you have advanced far in perfection, till you consider your-self the worst of all, and desire to be placed below all." And on this maxim the saint acted, and so have done all the. saints; St. Francis of Assisi, St. Mary Mag-dalene de Pazzi, and the rest, considered themselves the greatest sinners in the world, and were surprised that the earth sheltered them, and did not rather open under their feet to swallow them up alive; and they expressed themselves to this effect with the sincerest conviction, The Venerable Father John of Avila, who, from his earliest infancy had led a holy life, was on his deathbed; and the priest who came to attend him said many sub-lime things to him, taking him for what indeed he was, a great servant of God and a learned man; but Father Avila thus spoke to him: "Father, I pray you to make the recommendation of my soul, as of the soul of a crim-inal condemned to death; for such I am." This is the opinion which saints entertain of themselves in life and death.

We, too, must act in this manner, if we would save our souls, and keep ourselves in the grace of God till death, reposing all our confidence in God alone. The proud man relies on his own strength, and falls on that account; but the humble man, by placing all his trust in God alone, stands firm and falls not, however violent and multiplied the temptations may be; for his watchword is: *I can do all things in Him that strengthens me.*1 The devil at one time tempts us to presumption, at another

time to diffidence; whenever he suggests to us that we
are in no danger of falling, then we should tremble the
more; for were God but for an instant to withdraw his
grace from us, we are lost. When, again, he tempts us
to diffidence, then let us turn to God, and thus address
him with great confidence: *In you, O Lord, have I hoped,*

1 "Omnia possum in eo qui me confortat." Phil. 4.13.

[361] *I shall never be confounded.*1 My God, in You I
have put all my hopes; I hope never to meet with confusion,
nor to be bereft of Your grace. We ought to exercise ourselves continually, even to the very last moments of our
life, in these acts of diffidence in ourselves and of confidence in God, always beseeching God to grant us humility.

But it is not enough, in order to be humble, to have
a lowly opinion of ourselves, and to consider ourselves
the miserable beings that we really are; the man who is
truly humble, says Thomas a Kempis,2 despises himself,
and wishes also to be despised by others. This is what
Jesus Christ so earnestly recommends us to practice,
after his example: *Learn of Me, because I am meek and
humble of heart.*3 Whoever styles himself the greatest
sinner in the world, and then is angry when others despise him, plainly shows humility of tongue, but not of
heart. St. Thomas Aquinas says that a person who resents being slighted may be certain that he is far distant
from perfection, even though he should work miracles.
The divine Mother sent St. Ignatius Loyola from heaven
to instruct St. Mary Magdalene de Pazzi in humility;
and behold the lesson which the saint gave her: "Humility is a gladness at whatever leads us to despise our
selves."4 Mark well, a gladness; if the feelings are
stirred with resentment at the contempt we receive, at

least let us be glad in spirit.

And how is it possible for a soul not to love contempt, if she loves Jesus Christ, and beholds how her God was buffeted and spit upon, and how he suffered in his Passion! *Then did they spit in His face and buffeted Him; and*

1 "In te, Domine, speravi; non confundar in aeternum." Ps. 30.2.
2 *Imitation of Christ,* Bk. 3, ch. 7.
3 "Discite a me, quia mitis sum et humilis corde." Matt. 11.29.
4 *Cepar.* ch. 11.

[362] *others struck His face with the palms of their hands.*1 For this purpose our Redeemer wishes us to keep his image exposed on our altars, not indeed representing him in glory, but nailed to the cross, that we might have his disgraces constantly before our eyes; a sight which made the saints rejoice at being vilified in this world. And such was the prayer which St. John of the Cross addressed to Jesus Christ, when he appeared to him with the cross upon his shoulders: "O Lord, let me suffer, and be despised for You!"2 My Lord, on be holding You so reviled for my love, I only ask of You to let me suffer and be despised for Your love.

St. Francis de Sales said,3 "To support injuries is the touchstone of humility and of true virtue." If a person pretending to spirituality practices prayer, frequent Communion, fasts, and mortifies himself, and yet cannot put up with an insult, or a biting word, of what is it a sign? It is a sign that he is a hollow cane, without humility and without virtue. And what indeed can a soul do that loves Jesus Christ, if she is unable to endure a slight for the love of Jesus Christ, who has endured so much for her? Thomas a. Kempis, in his golden little

book of the Imitation of Christ, writes as follows:
"Since you have such an abhorrence of being humbled,
it is a sign that you are not dead to the world, have no
humility, and that you do not keep God before your
eyes. He that has not God before his eyes, is disturbed
at every syllable of censure that he hears."4 You cannot
endure being being beaten for God; endure at least a
passing word.

Oh, what surprise and scandal does that person occa-

1 "Tunc exspuerunt in faciem ejus, et colaphis eum ceciderunt; alii
autem palmas in faciem ejus dederunt." Matt. 26.67.
2 "Domine, pati et contemni pro te."
3 *Spirit of St Francis de Sales, ch.* 10.
4 *Imitation of Christ,* Bk. 3, ch. 46.

[363] sion, who communicates often, and then is ready
to resent every little word of contempt! On the contrary,
what edification does a soul give that answers insults
with words of mildness, spoken in order to conciliate the
offender; or perhaps makes no reply at all, nor com-
plains of it to others, but continues with placid looks,
and without showing the least sign of indignation! St.
John Chrysostom says that a meek person is not only
serviceable to himself but likewise to others, by the good
example he sets them of meekness in bearing contempt:
"The meek man is useful to himself and to others.1
Thomas a Kempis mentions, with regard to this subject,
several things in which we should practice humility; he
says as follows: "What others say shall command an
attentive hearing, and what you say shall be taken no
notice of. Others shall make a request and obtain it;
you shall ask for something and meet with a refusal.
Others shall be magnified in the mouths of men, and on

you no one shall bestow a word. Such and such an office shall be conferred on others, but you shall be passed by as unfit for anything. With such like trials the Lord will often prove his faithful servant; and to see how far he has learned to overcome himself and to hold his peace. Nature, indeed, will at times not like it; but you will derive immense profit thereby, if you support all in silence."2

It was a saying of St. Jane of Chantal, that "a person who is truly humble takes occasion from receiving some humiliation to humble himself the more."3 Yes, for he who is truly humble never supposes himself humbled as much as he deserves. Those who behave in this manner are styled blessed by Jesus Christ. They are not called blessed who are esteemed by the world, who are honored

1 "Mansuetus utilis sibi et aliis."
2 Bk. 3, ch. 49.
3 *Marsol.*, Bk. 4, ch. 8.

[364] and praised, as noble, as learned, as powerful; but they who are spoken ill of by the world, who are persecuted and calumniated; for it is for such that a glorious reward is prepared in heaven, if they only bear all with patience: *Blessed are you when they shall revile you and persecute you, and speak all that is evil against you untruly for My sake: be glad and rejoice, for your reward is very great in heaven.*1

The grand occasion for practicing humility is when we receive correction for some fault from Superiors or from others. Some people resemble the hedgehog: they seem all calmness and meekness as long as they remain untouched; but no sooner does a Superior or a friend touch them, by an observation on something which they have done imperfectly, than they immediately become all offended, and answer heatedly, that so and so is not true, or that they were right in doing so, or that such a correction is quite uncalled for. In a word, to rebuke them is to become their enemy; they behave like a person who raves at the surgeon for hurting them in the cure of their wounds. "He is angry with the surgeon,"[2] writes St. Bernard. "When the virtuous and humble man is corrected for a fault," says St. John Chrysostom, "he grieves for having committed it; the proud man on the other hand, on receiving correction, grieves also; but he grieves that his fault is detected; and on this account he is troubled, gives answers, and is angry with the person who corrects him." This is the golden rule given by St. Philip Neri, to be observed with regard to receiving correction: "Whoever would really become a saint must never excuse himself, although what is laid to his charge be not true."[3] And

---

1 "Beati estis, cum maledixerint vobis, et persecuti vos fuerint, et dixerint omne malum adversum vos mentientes, propter me; gaudete et exultate, quoniam merces vestra copiosa est in coelis." Matt. 5.11.
2 "Medicanti irascitur." *On the Song of Songs*, sermon 42.
3 *Bacci*, Bk. 2, ch. 17.

---

[365] there is only one case to be excepted from this rule, and that is when self-defense may appear necessary to prevent scandal. Oh, what merit with God has that soul that is wrongfully accused, and yet keeps silence, and refrains from defending itself! St. Teresa said: "There are occasions when a soul makes more progress and acquires a greater degree of perfection by refraining from excusing herself than by listening to ten sermons; because by not excusing herself she begins to

obtain freedom of spirit, and to be heedless whether the world speaks well or ill of her."1

Affections and Prayers

O Incarnate Word! I entreat You, by the merits of Your holy humility, which led You to embrace so many outrages and injuries for our love, deliver me from all pride, and grant me a share of Your humility. And what right have I to complain of any insult whatever that may be offered me, after having so often deserved hell? O my Jesus, by the merit of all the scorn and insults endured for me in Your Passion, grant me the grace to live and die humbled on this earth, as You did live and die humbled for my sake. For Your love I would willingly be despised and forsaken by all the world; but without You I can do nothing. I love You, O my sovereign good; I love You, O beloved of my soul! I love You; and I hope, through You, to fulfill my resolve of suffering all for You, insults, betrayals, persecutions, afflictions, dryness, and desolation; enough is it for me if You do not forsake me, O sole object of the love of my soul. Permit me never more to separate myself from You. Enkindle in me the desire to please You. Grant me fervor in loving You. Give me peace of mind in suffering for You. Give me resignation in all contradictions. Have mercy on me. I deserve nothing; but I fix all my hopes in You, who have purchased me with Your own blood.

And I hope all from you, too, O my Queen and my Mother Mary, who are the refuge of sinners!

1 *Way of Perfection*, ch. 16.

CHAPTER 6

LOVE IS NOT AMBITIOUS
(No Ulterior Motives)
(Charitas non est ambitiosa)

He that loves Jesus Christ desires Nothing but Jesus Christ

[366] HE that loves God does not desire to be esteemed and loved by his fellow-men: the single desire of his heart is to enjoy the favor of Almighty God, who alone forms the object of his love. St. Hilary writes, that all honor paid by the world is the business of the devil.1 And so it is; for the enemy traffics for hell, when he infects the soul with the desire of esteem; because, by thus laying aside humility, she runs great risks of plunging into every vice. St. James writes, that as God confers his graces with open hands upon the humble, so does he close them against the proud, whom he resists. *God resists the proud, and gives His grace to the humble.*2 He says he resists the proud, signifying that he does not even listen to their prayers. And certainly, among the acts of pride we may reckon the desire to be honored by men, and self-exaltation at receiving honors from them.

We have a frightful example of this in the history of Brother Justin the Franciscan, who had even risen to a lofty state of contemplation; but because perhaps and indeed without a perhaps he nourished within himself a desire of human esteem, behold what befell him. One day Pope Eugenius IV. sent for him; and on account of the great opinion he had of his sanctity, showed him

1 "Omnis saeculi honor diaboli negotium est." *In Matt.* ch. 3, n. 5.

"Deus superbis resistit; humilibus autem dat gratiam." James 4.6.

[367] peculiar marks of honor, embraced him, and made him sit by his side. Such high honors filled Brother Justin full of self-conceit; on which St. John Capistrano said to him, "Alas, Brother Justin, you did leave us an angel, and you return a devil!" And in fact, the hapless Brother becoming daily more and more puffed up with arrogance, and insisting on being treated according to his own estimate of himself, he at last murdered a brother with a knife; he afterwards became an apostate, and fled into the kingdom of Naples, where he perpetrated other atrocities; and there he died in prison, an apostate to the last.

Hence it is that a certain great servant of God wisely said, that when we hear or read of the fall of some towering cedars of Lebanon, of a Solomon, a Tertullian, an Osius, who had all the reputation of saints, it is a sign that they were not given wholly to God; but nourished inwardly some spirit of pride and so fell away. Let us therefore tremble, when we feel arise within us an ambition to appear in public, and to be esteemed by the world; and when the world pays us some tribute of honor, let us beware of taking complacency in it, which might prove the cause of our utter ruin.

Let us especially be on our guard against all ambitious seeking of preference, and sensibility in points of honor. St. Teresa said, "Where punctiliousness prevails, there spirituality will never prevail."1 Many persons make profession of a spiritual life, but they are worshippers of self. They have the semblance of certain virtues, but they are ambitious of being praised in all their undertakings; and if nobody else praises them, they praise themselves : in short, they strive to appeal-better than others; and if their honor be touched, they lose their peace, they leave off Holy Communion, they

1 *Way of Perfection*, ch. 13.

[368] omit all their devotions, and find no rest till they imagine they have got back their former standing. The true lovers of God do not so behave. They not only care-fully shun every word of self-esteem and all self-com-placency, but, further, they are sorry at hearing them selves commended by others, arid their gladness is to behold themselves held in small repute by the rest of men.

The saying of St. Francis of Assisi is most true : "What I am before God, that I am." Of what use is it to pass for great in the eyes of the world, if before God we be vile and worthless? And on- the contrary, what matters it to be despised by the world, provided we be dear and acceptable in the eyes of God? St. Augustine thus writes: "The approbation of him who praises neither heals a bad conscience, nor does the reproach of one who blames wound a good conscience."1 As the man who praises us cannot deliver us from the chastise-ment of our evil doings, so neither can he who blames us rob us of the merit of our good actions. "What does it matter," says St. Teresa, "though we be condemned and reviled by creatures, if before You, O God! we are great and without blame?" The saints had no other desire than to live unknown, and to pass for contemptible in the estimation of all. Thus writes St. Francis de Sales : "But what wrong do we suffer when people have a bad opinion of us, since we ought to have such of ourselves?

Perhaps we know that we are bad, and yet wish to pass off for good in the estimation of others."2

Oh, what security is found in the hidden life for such as wish cordially to love Jesus Christ! Jesus Christ himself set us the example, by living hidden and despised for thirty years in a workshop. And with the same view

1 "Nec malam conscientiam sanat laudantis praeconium, nec bonam vulnerat conviciantis opprobrium." *Contra Petil.* Bk. 3, ch. 7.
2 *Spirit of St Francis de Sales*, ch. 3.

[369] of escaping the esteem of men, the saints went and hid themselves in deserts and in caves. It was said by St. Vincent de Paul, 1 that a love of appearing in public, and of being spoken of in terms of praise, and of hearing our conduct commended, or that people should say that we succeed admirably and work wonders, is an evil which, while it makes us unmindful of God, contaminates our best actions, and proves the most fatal drawback to the spiritual life.

Whoever, therefore, would make progress in the love of Jesus Christ, must absolutely give a death-blow to the love of self-esteem. But how shall we inflict this blow? Behold how St. Mary Magdalene de Pazzi instructs us : "That which keeps alive the appetite for self-esteem is the occupying a favorable position in the minds of all; consequently the death of self-esteem is to keep one's self hidden, so as not to be known to any one. And till we learn to die in this manner, we shall never be true servants of God."2

In order, then, to be pleasing in the sight of God, we must avoid all ambition of appearing and of making a parade in the eyes of men. And we must shun with still greater caution the ambition of governing others. Sooner than behold this accursed ambition set foot in the convent, St. Teresa 3 declared she would prefer to have the whole convent burned, and all the nuns with it. So that she signified her wish, that if ever one of her religious should be caught aiming at the Superiorship, she should be expelled from the community, or at least undergo perpetual confinement. St. Mary Magdalene de Pazzi said, "The honor of a spiritual person consists in being put below all, and in abhorring all superiority over others. The ambition of a soul that loves God should be to excel all others in humility, according to

1 *Abelly*, Bk. 3, ch. 34, 48.
2 *Cepar.* ch. 13.
3 *Way of Perfection,* ch. 8.

[370] the counsel of St. Paul : *In humility let each esteem others better than themselves.*1 In a word, he that loves God must make God the sole object of his ambition.

Affections and Prayers

My Jesus, grant me the ambition of pleasing You, and make me forget all creatures and myself also. What will it profit me to be loved by the whole world, if I be not loved by You, the only love of my soul! My Jesus, You earnest into the world to win our hearts; if I am unable to give You my heart, do You please to take it and replenish it with Your love, and never allow me to be separated from You any more. I have, alas! turned my back upon You in the past; but now that I am con- scious of the evil I have done, I grieve over it with my whole heart, and no affliction in the world can so distress me, as the remembrance of the offenses that I have so often committed against You. I am consoled to think that You are infinite goodness, that You do not disdain to love a sinner who loves You. My beloved Redeemer, O sweetest love of my soul, I have heretofore slighted You; but now at least I love You more than myself! I offer You myself and all that belongs to me. I have only the one wish to love You, and to please You. This forms all my ambition; accept of it, and be pleased to increase it, and exterminate in me all desire of earthly goods. You are indeed deserving of love, and great indeed are my obligations of loving You. Behold me then, I wish to be wholly Your; and I will suffer whatever You please, You who for love of me did die of sorrow on the cross! You wish me to be a saint; You can make me a saint; in You I place my trust.

And I also confide in your protection, O Mary, great Mother of God!

1 "In humilitate superiores." Phil. 2.3.

CHAPTER 7

LOVE IS NOT SELF-SEEKING
(Detachment)
(*Charitas non quaerit quae sua sunt*)

He that loves Jesus Christ seeks to detach Himself from every Creature

[371] WHOEVER desires to love Jesus Christ with his whole heart must banish from his heart all that is not God, but is merely self-love. This is the meaning of those words, "seeks not her own;" not to seek ourselves, but only what pleases God. And this is what God requires of us all, when he says: *You shall love the Lord your God with your whole heart*.1 Two things are needful to love God with our whole heart: **1.** To clear it of earth. **2.** To fill it with holy love. It follows, that a heart in which any earthly affections linger can never belong wholly to God. St. Philip Neri 2 said, "that as much love as we bestow on the creature, is so much taken from the Creator." In the next place, how must the earth be purged away from the heart? Truly by mortification and detachment from creatures. Some souls complain that they seek God, and do not find him; let them listen to what St. Teresa says: "Wean your heart from creatures, and seek God, and you will find him."3

The mistake is, that some indeed wish to become saints, but after their own fashion; they would love Jesus Christ, but in their own way, without forsaking those diversions, that vanity of dress, those delicacies in food : they love God, but if they do not succeed in ob-

1 "Diliges Dominum Deum tuum ex toto corde tuo." Matt. 22.37.

2 *Bacci*, Bk. 22, ch. 15.
3 *Avis*, 36.

[372] taining such or such an office, they live discontented;
if, too, they happen to be touched in point of esteem, they
are all on fire; if they do not recover from an illness,
they lose all patience. They love God; but they refuse
to let go that attachment for the riches, the honors of
the world, for the vainglory of being reckoned of good
family, of great learning, and better than others. Such
as these practice prayer, and frequent Holy Communion; but inasmuch as they take with them hearts full of
earth, they derive little profit. Our Lord does not even
speak to them, for he knows that it is but a waste of
words. In fact, he said as much to St. Teresa on a certain occasion: "I would speak to many souls, but the
world keeps up such a noise about their ears, that my
voice would never be heard by them. Oh, that they
would retire a little from the world!" Whosoever, then,
is full of earthly affections cannot even so much as hear
the voice of God that speaks to him. But unhappy the
man that continues attached to the sensible goods of this
earth; he may easily become so blinded by them as one
day to quit the love of Jesus Christ; and for want of
forsaking these transitory goods he may lose God, the
infinite good, forever. St. Teresa said: "It is a reasonable consequence, that he who runs after perishable goods
should himself perish."

St. Augustine1 informs us that Tiberius Caesar desired that the Roman senate should enroll Jesus Christ
among the rest of their gods; but the senate refused to
do so, on the ground that he was too proud a God, and
would be worshiped alone without any companions.
It is quite true : God will be alone the object of our ad-

oration and love; not indeed from pride, but because it
is his just due, and because too of the love he bears us.
For as he himself loves us exceedingly, he desires in re-

1 *On the Consolation of the Gospel*, Bk. 1, ch. 12.

[373] turn all our love; and is therefore jealous of any one
else sharing the affections of our hearts, of which he desires to be the sole possessor: "Jesus is a jealous lover,"1
says St. Jerome; and he is unwilling therefore for us to
fix our affections on anything but himself. And when
ever he beholds any created object taking a share of our
hearts, he looks on it as it were with jealousy, as the
Apostle St. James says, because he will not endure a
rival, but will remain the sole object of all our love: Do
you think that the Scripture says in vain: *With envy does
the Spirit desire which dwells in you*?2 The Lord in the
sacred Canticles praises his spouse, saying: *My sister,
my spouse, is a garden enclosed.*3 He calls her a garden
enclosed," because the soul that is his spouse keeps her
heart shut against every earthly love, in order to preserve
all for Jesus Christ alone. And does Jesus Christ per-
chance not deserve all our love? Ah, too much, too
much has he deserved it, both for his own goodness and
for his love towards us. The saints knew this well, and
for this reason St. Francis de Sales said: "Were I conscious of one fiber in my heart that did not belong to
God, I would immediately tear it out."4

David longed to have wings free from all lime of
worldly affections, in order to fly away and repose in
God : *Who will give me wings like a dove, and I will fly
and be at rest?*5 Many souls would wish to see them
selves released from every earthly trammel to fly to God,
and would in reality make lofty flights in the way of

sanctity, if they would but detach themselves from

1 "Zelotypus est Jesus." *Letter to Eustochium.*
2 "An putatis quoniam inaniter Scriptura dicat : Ad invidiam con-
cupiscit Spiritus qui habitat in vobis?" James 4.5.
3 "Hortus conclusus soror mea, Sponsa." Song of Songs, 4.12.
4 *Spirit of St Francis de Sales*, ch. 9.
5 "Quis dabit mihi pennas sicut columbae, et volabo, et requies-
cam?" Ps. 54.7.

[374] everything in this world; but whereas they retain some
little immoderate affection, and will not use violence with
themselves to get rid of it, they remain always languishing on in their misery, without ever so much as lifting a
foot from the ground. St. John of the Cross said: "The
soul that remains with its affections attached to any
thing, however small, will, notwithstanding many virtues
which it may possess, never arrive at divine union; for
it signifies little whether the bird be tied by a slight
thread or a thick one; since, however slight it may be,
provided she does not break it, she remains always
bound, and unable to fly. Oh, what a pitiful thing it is
to see certain souls, rich in spiritual exercises, in virtues
and divine favors; yet, because they are not bold enough
to break off some trifling attachment, they cannot attain
to divine union, for which it only needed one strong and
resolute flight to break effectively that fatal thread!
Since, when once the soul is emptied of all affection to
creatures, God cannot help communicating himself
wholly to it."1

He who would possess God entirely must give himself
up entirely to God: *My beloved to me and I to him*,2 says
the Sacred Spouse. My beloved has given himself entirely to me, and I give myself entirely to him. The
love which Jesus Christ bears us causes him to desire

all our love; and without all he is not satisfied. On this account we find St. Teresa thus writing to the Prioress of one of her convents: "Endeavor to train souls to a total detachment from everything created, because they are to be trained to be the spouses of a king so jealous, that he would have them even forget themselves." St. Mary Magdalene de Pazzi took a little book of devotion from one of her novices, merely because she observed that she was too much attached to it. Many souls ac-

1 *Ascent of Mount Carmel*, Bk. 1. ch. 11.
2 "Dilectus meus mihi, et ego illi." Song of Songs, 2.16.

[375] quit themselves of the duty of prayer, of visiting the Blessed Sacrament, of frequenting Holy Communion; but nevertheless they make little or no progress in perfection, and all because they keep some fondness for something in their heart; and if they persist in living thus, they will not only be always miserable, but run the risk of losing all.

We must, therefore, beseech Almighty God, with David, to rid our heart of all earthly attachments: *Create a clean heart in me, O God.*1 Otherwise we can never be wholly his. He has given us to understand very plainly, that whoever will not renounce everything in this world, cannot be his disciple: *Every one of you that does not renounce all that he possesses cannot be my disciple.*2 For this reason the ancient Fathers of the desert were accustomed first to put this question to any youth who desired to associate himself with them : "Do you bring an empty heart, that the Holy Spirit may fill it?" Our Lord said the same thing to St. Gertrude, when she besought him to signify what he wished of her: "I wish nothing else, he said, but to find a heart devoid of crea-

tures."3 We must therefore say to God with great resolution and courage: O Lord, I prefer You to all; to
health, to riches, to honors and dignities, to applause, to
learning, to consolations, to high hopes, to desires, and
even to the very graces and gifts which I may receive of
You! In short, I prefer You to every created good
which is not You, O my God. Whatever benefit You
grant me, O my God, nothing besides Yourself will
satisfy me. I desire You alone, and nothing else.

When the heart is detached from creatures, the divine
love immediately enters and fills it. Moreover, St. Teresa

1 "Cor mundum crea in me, Deus." Ps. 1.12.
2 "Qui non renuntiat omnibus quae possidet, non potest meus esse
discipulus." Luke 14.33.
3 *Revelations*, Bk. 4, ch. 26.

[376] said: "As soon as evil occasions are removed, the
heart immediately turns itself to love God." Yes, for the
human heart cannot exist without loving; it must either
love the Creator or creatures: if it does not love creatures, then assuredly it will love God. In short, we
must leave all in order to gain all. "All for all,"1 says
Thomas a Kempis. As long as St. Teresa cherished a certain affection, though pure, towards one of her relatives,
she did not wholly belong to God; but when afterwards
she summoned courage, and resolutely cut off the attachment, then she deserved to hear these words from
Jesus: "Now, Teresa, you are all mine, and I am all
thine."2 One heart is quite too small to love this God,
so loving and so lovely, and who merits an infinite love;
and shall we then think of dividing this one little heart
between creatures and God? The Venerable Louis da
Ponte felt ashamed to speak thus to God: "O Lord, I

love You above all things, above riches, honors, friends, relatives;" for it seemed to him as much as to say: "O Lord, I love You more than dirt, than smoke, and the worms of the earth!"

The Prophet Jeremiah says that the Lord is all good ness towards him who seeks him : *The Lord is good to the soul that seeks him.*3 But he understands it of a soul that seeks God alone. O blessed loss! O blessed gain! to lose worldly goods, which cannot satisfy the heart and are soon gone, in order to obtain the sovereign and eternal good, which is God! It is related that a pious hermit, one day while the king was hunting through the wood, began to run to and fro as if in search of something; the king, observing him thus oc-cupied, inquired of him who he was and what he was doing; the hermit replied: "And may I ask your majesty

1 "Totum pro toto." *Imitation of Christ*, Bk. 3, ch. 37.
2 *Life*, ch. 39.
3 "Bonus est Dominus . . animae quaerenti illum." Lam. 3.25.

[377] what you are engaged about in this desert?" The king made answer: "I am going in pursuit of game." And the hermit replied: "I, too, am going in pursuit of God." With these words he continued his road and went away. During the present life this must likewise be our only thought, our only purpose, to go in search of God in or-der to love him, and in search of his will in order to ful-fill it, ridding our heart of all love of creatures. And whenever some worldly good would present itself to our imaginations to solicit our love, let us be ready prepared with this answer: "I have despised the kingdom of this world, and all the charms of this life, for the sake of the love of my Lord Jesus Christ."1 And what else are all

the dignities and grandeurs of this world but smoke, filth, and vanity, which all disappear at death? Blessed he who can say: "My Jesus, I have left all for Your love; You are my only love; You alone are sufficient for me."

Ah, when once the love of God takes full possession of a soul, she of her own accord (supposing always, of course, the assistance of divine grace) strives to divest herself of everything that could prove a hindrance to her belonging wholly to God. St. Francis de Sales remarks that when a house catches fire, all the furniture is thrown out of the window; 2 meaning thereby, that when a person gives himself entirely to God, he needs no persuasion of preachers or confessors, but of his own accord seeks to get rid of every earthly affection. Father Segneri the younger called divine love a robber, which happily despoils us of all, that we may come into possession of God alone. A certain man, of respectable position in life, having renounced everything in order to become poor for the love of Jesus Christ, was questioned by a

1 "Regnum mundi et omnem ornatum saeculi contempsi, propter amorem Domini mei Jesu Christi." *Offic. nec Virg. nec Mart.* resp. 8.
2 *Spirit of St Francis de Sales*, ch. 27.

[378] friend how he fell into such a state of poverty; he took from his pocket a small volume of the Gospels, and said: "Behold, this is what has stripped me of all." The Holy Spirit says: *If a man shall give all the substance of his house for love, he shall despise it as nothing.* 1 And when a soul has her whole love in God, she despises all, wealth, pleasures, dignities, territories, kingdoms, and all her longing is after God alone; she says, again and again: "My God, I wish for You only, and nothing more." St.

Francis de Sales writes: "The pure love of God consumes everything which is not God, to convert all into
itself; for whatever we do for the love of God is love."2

The Sacred Spouse said: He brought me into the cellar
of wine, he set in order love in me.3 This cellar of wine,
writes St. Teresa, is divine love, which, on taking possession of a soul, so perfectly inebriates it as to make it forgetful of everything created. A person intoxicated is,
as it were, dead in his senses; he does not see, nor hear,
nor speak; and so it happens to the soul inebriated with
divine love. She has no longer any sense of the things
of the world; she wishes to think only of God, to speak
only of God; she recognizes no other motive in all her actions but to love and to please God. In the sacred Canticles the Lord forbids them to awake his beloved, who
sleeps: *Stir not up, nor make the beloved to awake, till she
please.*4 This blessed sleep, enjoyed by souls espoused
to Jesus Christ, says St. Basil, is nothing else than "the
utter oblivion of all things,"5 a virtuous and voluntary
forgetfulness of every created thing, in order to be occu-

1 "Si dederit homo omnem substantiam domus suae pro dilectione,
quasi nihil despiciet eam." Song of Songs, 8.7.
2 *Letters* 531, 203.
3 "Introduxit me in cellam vinariam, ordinavit in me charitatem."
Song of Songs, 2.4.
4 "Ne suscitetis, neque evigilare faciatis dilectam." Song of Songs,
2.7.
5 "Summa rerum omnium oblivio." *Reg. fus. disp. int.* 6.

[379] pied solely with God, and to be able to exclaim with
St. Francis, "My God and my all."1 My God, what are
riches, and dignities, and goods of the world, compared
with You! You are my all and my every good. "My God
and my all." Thomas a Kempis writes,2 "Oh, sweet word!

It speaks enough for him who understands it; and to him who loves, it is most delicious to repeat again and again: My God and my all, my God and my all! "

Detachment from Relatives, above all, in regard to one's Vocation

Wherefore, to arrive at perfect union with God, a total detachment from creatures is of absolute necessity. And to come to particulars, we must divest ourselves of all disordered affection towards relatives. Jesus Christ says :
*If any man come to Me and hate not his father and mother, and wife and children, and brethren and sisters, yes, and his own life also, he cannot be My disciple.*3 And wherefore this hatred to relatives? because generally, as regards the interests of the soul, we cannot have greater enemies than our own kindred: *And a man's enemies shall be those of his own household.*4

1 "Deus meus, et omnia."
2 *Imitation of Christ* Bk. 3, ch. 34.
3 "Si quis venit ad me, et non odit patrem suum, et matrem, et uxorem, et filios, et sorores, adhuc autem et animam suam, non potest meus esse discipulus." Luke 14.26.
4 "Et inimici hominis domestici ejus." Matt. 10.36.

[pp. 380-386, on the priesthood, omitted]

Detachment from Human Respect and from Self-will

[387] Moreover, any one that would belong wholly to God must be free of all human respect. Oh, how many souls does this accursed respect keep aloof from God, and even separate them from him forever! For instance, if they hear mention made of some or other of their fail-

ings, oh, what do they not do to justify themselves, and to convince the world that it is a calumny! If they perform some good work, how industrious are they to circulate it everywhere! They would have it known to the whole world, in order to be universally applauded. The saints behave in a very different way : they would rather publish their defects to the whole world, in order to pass in the eyes of all for the miserable creatures which they really are in their own eyes; and, on the contrary, in practicing any act of virtue, they prefer to have God alone know of it; for their only care is to be acceptable to him. It is on this account that so many of them were enchanted with solitude, mindful, as they were, of the words of Jesus Christ : *But when you give alms, let not your left hand know what your right hand does.*1 And again: *But you, when you shall pray, enter into your room; and having shut the door, pray to your Father in secret.*2

1 "Te autem faciente eleemosynam, nesciat sinistra tua quid faciat dextera tua." Matt. 6.3.
2 "Cum oraveris, intra in cubiculum tuum, et clause ostio, ora Patrem tuum in abscondito." Matt. 6.6.

[388] But of all things, self-detachment is most needful; that is, detachment from self-will. Only once succeed in subduing yourself, and you will easily triumph in every other combat. *Vince teipsum,* "Conquer yourself," was the maxim which St. Francis Xavier inculcated on all. And Jesus Christ said : *If any one would come after Me, let him deny himself.*1 Behold in summary all that we need practice to become saints; to deny our selves, and not to follow our own will : *Go not after your lusts, but turn away from your own will.*2 And this is the greatest grace, said St. Francis of Assisi, that we can receive from God : the power, namely, to conquer our

selves by denying self-will. St. Bernard writes, that if
all men would resist self-will, none would ever be
damned : "Let self-will cease, and there will be no
hell."3 The same saint writes, that it is the baneful
effect of self-will to contaminate even our good works:
"Self-will is a great evil, since it renders your good works
no longer good."4 As, for instance, were a penitent obstinately bent on mortifying himself, or on fasting, or
on taking the discipline against the will of his director;
we see that this act of penance, done at the instigation
of self-will, becomes very defective.

Unhappy the man that lives as the slave of self-will! for
he shall have a yearning for many things, and shall not
possess them; while, on the other hand, he will be forced
to undergo many things distasteful and bitter to his inclinations: *From whence are wars and contentions among
you? Are they not from your concupiscences, which*

1 "Si quis vult post me venire, abneget semetipsum." Matt. 16.24.
2 "Post concupiscentias tuas non eas, et a voluntate tua avertere."
Ecclus. (Sirach) 18.30.
3 "Cesset voluntas propria, et infernus non erit." *In Temp. Pasch.*
sermon 3.
4 "Grande malum propria voluntas, qua fit ut bona tua tibi bona non
sint." *On the Song of Songs,* sermon 71.

[389] *war in your members? You covet, and have not.*1
The first war springs from the appetite for sensual delights.
Let us take away the occasion; let us mortify the eyes; let
us recommend ourselves to God, and the war will be over.
The second war arises from the covetousness of riches:
let us cultivate a love of poverty, and this war will cease.
The third war has its source in ambitiously seeking after
honors : let us love humility and the hidden life, and this
war too will be no more. The fourth war, and the most

ruinous of all, comes from self-will : let us practice resignation in all things which happen by the will of God, and the war will cease. St. Bernard tells us that whenever we see a person troubled, the origin of his trouble is nothing else but his inability to gratify self-will. "Whence comes disquiet," says the saint, "except that we follow self-will?"2 Our Blessed Lord once complained of this to St. Mary Magdalene de Pazzi, in these words : "Certain souls desire my Spirit, but after their own fancy; and so they become incapable of receiving it."

We must therefore love God in the way that pleases God, and not that pleases us. God will have the soul divested of all, in order to be united to himself, and to be replenished with his divine love. St. Teresa 3 writes as follows : "The prayer of union appears to me to be nothing more than to die utterly, as it were, to all things in this world, for the enjoyment of God alone. One thing is certain, that the more completely we empty ourselves of creatures, by detaching ourselves from them for the love of God, the more abundantly will he fill us with himself, and the more closely shall we be united with

1 "Unde bella et lites in vobis? nonne hinc, ex concupiscentiis vestris, quae militant in membris vestris? Concupiscitis, et non habetis." James 4.1,2.
2 "Unde turbatio, nisi quod propriam sequimur voluntatem?" *De Div.*, sermon 26.
3 *Interior Castle*, ch. 1.

[390] him." Many spiritual persons would attain to union with God; but then they do not desire the adversities which God sends them: they fret at having to suffer from ill-health, from poverty, from insults; but, for lack of resignation, they will never come to a perfect

union with God. Let us hear what St. Catherine of Genoa said: "To arrive at union with God, the adversities which God sends us are absolutely necessary; his purpose is, to consume in us, by means of them, all irregular movements, both within and without. And hence all contempt, ailments, poverty, temptations, and other trials, are all indispensable, to give us the opportunity of fighting; that so, by the way of victory, we may eventually extinguish all disordered movements, so as to be no more sensible of them; furthermore, until we be gin to find contradictions sweet for God's sake, instead of bitter, we shall never arrive at divine union."

I here subjoin the practice of it, taught by St. John of the Cross. The saint says that in order to [attain] perfect union, "a thorough mortification of the senses and of the appetites is necessary. On the part of the senses, every single relish that presents itself to them, if it be not purely for the glory of God, should immediately be rejected for the love of Jesus Christ; for example, should you have a desire to see or hear something in no way conducive to the greater glory of God, then refrain from it. As to the appetites also, endeavor to force ourselves always to choose the worst, the most disagreeable, or the poorest, without fostering any other wish than to suffer and to be despised."1
In a word, he that truly loves Jesus Christ loses all affection for things of earth, and seeks to strip himself of all, in order to keep himself united with Jesus Christ alone. Jesus is the object of all his desires, Jesus the subject of all his thoughts; for Jesus he continually

1 *Ascent of Mount Carmel*, Bk. 1, ch. 4-13.

[391] sighs; in every place, at every time, on every occa-

sion, his sole aim is to give pleasure to Jesus. But to reach this point, we must study unceasingly to rid the heart of every affection which is not for God. And, I ask, what is meant by giving the soul entirely to God? It means, first, to shun whatever may be displeasing to God, and to do what is most pleasing to him; secondly, it means to accept unreservedly all that comes from his hands, however hard or disagreeable it may be; it means, thirdly, to give the preference in all things to the will of God over our own: this is what is meant by belonging wholly to God.

Affections and Prayers

Ah, my God and my all! I cannot help feeling that, in spite of all my ingratitude and neglect in Your service, You still invite me to love You. Behold me, then; I will resist You no longer. I will leave all to be wholly Yours. I will no more live for myself: Your claims on my love are too strong. My soul is enamored of You; my Jesus, it sighs after You. And how can I possibly love anything else, after seeing You die of sufferings on a cross in order to save me! how could I behold You dead, and exhausted with torments, and not love You with my whole heart? Yes, I love You indeed with all my soul; and I have no other desire but to love You in this life and for all eternity. My love, my hope, my courage, and my consolation, give me strength to be faithful to You; grant me light, and make known to me from what I ought to detach myself; supply me too with a strong will to obey You in all things. O love of my soul! I offer myself, and deliver myself up entirely,
to satisfy the desire which You have to unite Yourself to me, that I may be wholly united with You, my God and my all. Oh, come then, my Jesus; come and take possession of my whole self, and occupy all my thoughts and all my affections. I renounce all my appetites, all my comforts, and all created

things; You alone are sufficient for me. Grant me the grace to think only of You, to desire only You, to seek only You, my beloved and my only good!

O Mary, Mother of God, obtain for me holy perseverance!

CHAPTER 8

LOVE IS NOT PROVOKED TO ANGER
(Meekness)
(*Charitas non irritatur*)

He that loves Jesus Christ is never angry
with his Neighbor

[392] THE virtue not to be angry at the unpleasant things that happen to us is the daughter of meekness. We have already spoken at length of the acts which belong to meekness in preceding chapters; but since this is a virtue which requires to be constantly practiced by everyone living among his fellow-men, we will here make some remarks on the same subject more in particular, and more adapted for practice.

Humility and meekness were the favorite virtues of Jesus Christ; so that he bade his disciples learn of him to be meek and humble: *Learn of Me, for I am meek and humble of heart.* 1 Our Redeemer was called the Lamb, --*Behold the Lamb of God,* 2 -- as well in consideration of his having to be offered in sacrifice on the cross for our sins, as in consideration of the meekness exhibited by him during his entire life, but more especially at the time of his Passion. When in the house of Caiphas he received a blow from that servant, who at the same time upbraided him with presumption in those words: Do you answer the high-priest like that? Jesus only answered: *If I have spoken evil, give testimony of the evil; but if well, why do you strike me?*3 He observed the same invariable

1 "Discite a me quia mitis sum et humilis corde." Matt. 11.29.
2 "Ecce Agnus Dei." John 1.29.

3 "Si male locutus sum, testimonium perhibe de malo; si autem bene, quid me caedis?" John 18.23.

[393] meekness of conduct till death. While on the cross, and made the object of universal scorn and blasphemy, he only besought the Eternal Father to forgive them: *Father, forgive them; for they know not what they do.*1

Oh, how dear to Jesus Christ are those meek souls who, in suffering insults, derisions, calumnies, persecutions, and even chastisement and blows, are not irritated against the person that thus injures or strikes them: *The prayer of the meek has always pleased you.*2 God is always pleased with the prayers of the meek; that is to say, their prayers are always heard. Heaven is expressly promised to the meek: *Blessed are the meek, for they shall possess the land.*3 Father Alvarez said that paradise is the country of those who are despised and persecuted and trodden under foot, Yes, for it is for them that the possession of the eternal kingdom is reserved, and not for the haughty, who are honored and esteemed by the world. David declares that the meek shall not only inherit eternal happiness, but shall likewise enjoy great peace in the present life: *The meek shall inherit the land, and shall delight in abundance of peace.*4 It is so, because the saints harbor no malice against those who ill-treat them, but rather love them the more; and the Lord, in reward for their patience, gives them an increase of interior peace. St. Teresa said: "I seem to experience a renewed love towards those persons who speak ill of me."5 This gave occasion to the Sacred Congregation to say of the saint, that "even insults themselves supplied her with the food of love."6 Offenses became a fresh reason for

1 "Pater! dimitte illis; non enim sciunt quid faciunt." Luke 23.34.

2 "Mansuetorum semper tibi placuit deprecatio." Judith 9.16.
3 "Beati mites, quoniam ipsi possidebunt terram." Matt. 5.4.
4 "Mansueti autem haereditabunt terram, et delectabuntur in multitudine pacis." Ps. 36.11
5 *Rib.* Bk. 4, ch. 26
6 "Offensiones amoris ipsi escam ministrabunt."

[394] her to love the person who had offended her. No one can have such meekness as this, if he has not a great humility and a low opinion of himself, so as to consider himself worthy of every kind of contempt; and hence we see, on the contrary, that the proud are always irritable and vindictive, because they have a high conceit of themselves, and esteem themselves worthy of all honor. *Blessed are the dead who die in the Lord.*1 We must, indeed, die in the Lord to be blessed, and to enjoy that blessedness even in the present life: we mean, such happiness as can be had before entering heaven, which, though certainly much below that of heaven, yet far surpasses all the pleasures of sense in this world: *And the peace of God, which surpasses all under standing, keep your hearts;*2 so wrote the Apostle to his disciples. But to gain this peace, even in the midst of insults and calumnies, we must be dead in the Lord: a dead person, however much he may be ill-treated and trampled on by others, resents it not; in like manner, he who is meek, like a dead body, which no longer sees or feels, should endure all the outrages committed against him. Whoever loves Jesus Christ from his heart easily attains to this; because, as he is conformed in all things to his will, he accepts with equal composure and peace of mind prosperous and adverse occurrences, consolations and afflictions, injuries and courtesies. Such was the conduct of the Apostle; and he says, therefore: *I exceedingly abound with joy in all onr tribulation.*3 Oh, happy the man who reaches this point of virtue! he enjoys a continual peace, which is a

treasure precious beyond all other goods of this world. St. Francis de Sales said: "Of what value is the whole universe in comparison with peace of heart?"4 And, in

1 "Beati mortui qui in Domino moriuntur." Apoc. (Rev.) 14.13.
2 "Pax Dei, quae exsuperat omnem sensum." Phil. 4.7.
3 "Superabundo gaudio in omni tribulatione nostra." 2 Cor. 7.4
4 *Letter* 580.

[395] truth, of what avail are all riches and all the honors of the world to a man that lives in disquiet, and whose heart is not at peace?"

In short, in order to remain constantly united with Jesus Christ, we must do all with tranquility, and not be troubled at any contradiction that we may encounter. *The Lord is not in the earthquake.*1 The Lord does not abide in troubled hearts. Let us listen to the beautiful lessons given on this subject by that master of meekness St. Francis de Sales: "Never put yourself in a passion, nor open the door to anger on any pretext whatever; be cause, when once it has gained an entrance, it is no longer in our power to banish it, or moderate it, when we wish to do so. The remedies against it are: **1.** To check it immediately, by diverting the mind to some other object, and not to speak a word. **2.** To imitate the Apostles when they beheld the tempest at sea, and to have recourse to God, to whom it belongs to restore peace to the soul. **3.** If you feel that, owing to your weakness, anger has already got footing in your breast, in that case do yourself violence to regain your composure, and then try to make acts of humility and of sweetness towards the person against whom you are irritated; but all this must be done with sweetness and without violence, for it is of the utmost importance not to irritate the wounds."2 The

saint said that he himself was obliged to labor much during his life to overcome two passions which predomi-
nated in him, namely, anger and love: to subdue the
passion of anger, he avowed it had cost him twenty-two
years hard struggle, As to the passion of love, he had
succeeded in changing its object, by leaving creatures,
and turning all his affections to God. And in this
manner the saint acquired so great an interior peace,
that it was visible even in his exterior; for he was in-

1 "Non in commotione Deus." 1 Kings (1 Sam.) 19.11.
2 *Introduction to the Devout Life*, ch. 8.

[396] variably seen with a serene countenance and a smile
on his features.

*From where do wars come? . . . Are they not from your con-
cupiscences?*1 When we are made angry by some contradiction, we fancy we shall find relief and quiet by giving
vent to our anger in actions, or at least in words: but we
are mistaken, it is not so; for after having done so, we
shall find that we are much more disturbed than before.
Whoever desires to persevere in uninterrupted peace,
must beware of ever yielding to ill-humor. And when
ever any one feels himself attacked by this ill-humor, he
must do his utmost to banish it immediately; and he
must not go to rest with it in his heart, but must divert
himself from it by the perusal of some book, by singing
some devout canticle, or by conversing on some pleasant
subject with a friend, The Holy Spirit says: *Anger rests
in the bosom of a fool.*2 Anger remains a long time in the
heart of fools, who have little love for Jesus Christ; but
if by stealth it should ever enter into the hearts of the true
lovers of Jesus Christ, it is quickly dislodged, and does not
remain. A soul that cordially loves the Redeemer never

feels in a bad humor, because, as she desires only what God desires, she has all she wishes for, and consequently is ever tranquil and well-balanced. The divine will tranquil lizes her in every misfortune that occurs; and thus she is able at all times to observe meekness towards all. But we cannot acquire this meekness without a great love for Jesus Christ. In fact, we know by experience that we are not meeker and gentler towards others, except when we feel an increased tenderness towards Jesus Christ.

But since we cannot constantly experience this tender ness, we must prepare ourselves, in our mental prayer,

1 "Unde bella? . . . nonne hinc, ex concupiscentiis vestris?" James 4.1, 2.
2 "Ira in sinu stulti requiescit." Ecclus. (Sirach) 7.10.

[397] to bear the crosses that may befall us. This was the practice of the saints; and so they were ever ready to receive with patience and meekness injuries, blows, and chastisements. When we meet with an insult from our neighbor, unless we have frequently trained ourselves beforehand, we shall find it extremely difficult to know what course to take, in order not to yield to the force of anger; in the very moment, our passion will make it ap-pear but reasonable for us to retort boldly the audacity of the person who insults us, but St. John Chrysostom says that it is not the right way to quench the fire which is raging in the mind of our neighbor by the fire of an indignant reply; to do so will only enkindle it the more: "One fire is not extinguished by another."1

Some one may say: But why should I use courtesy and gentleness towards an impertinent fellow, that insults me without cause? But St. Francis de Sales replies: "We must practice meekness, not only with reason, but against reason."2

We must therefore endeavor, on such occasions, to make a kind answer; and in this way we shall allay the fire: *A mild answer dissolves wrath.* 3 But when the mind is troubled, the best expedient will be to keep silence. St. Bernard writes: "The eye troubled by anger sees not straight."4 When the eye is dimmed with passion, it no longer distinguishes between what is and what is not un- just; anger is like a veil drawn over the eyes, so that we can no longer discern between right and wrong; where- fore we must, like St. Francis de Sales, make a compact with our tongue: "I have made a covenant with my tongue," he wrote, "never to speak while my heart is disturbed."

1 "Igne non potest ignis extingui." On Genesis, homily 58.
2 *Letter* 231.
3 "Responsio mollis frangit iram." Prov. 15.1.
4 "Turbatus prae ira oculus . . . rectum non videt." *On Consideration,* Bk. 2, ch. 11.

[398] But there are moments when it seems absolutely nec- essary to check insolence with severe words. David said: *Be angry, and sin not.*1 Occasions do exist, therefore, when we may be lawfully angry, provided it be without sin. But here is just the matter: speculatively speaking, it seems expedient at times to speak and reply to some people in terms of severity, in order to make an impress- sion on them; but in practice it is very difficult to do this without some fault on our part; so that the sure way is always to admonish, or to reply, with gentleness, and to scrupulously guard against all resentment. St. Francis

de Sales said: "I have never been angry without afterwards repenting of it." And when, for some reason or other, we still feel warm, the safest way, as I said before, is to keep silence, and reserve the remonstrance till a more convenient moment, when the heart is cooled down.

We ought particularly to observe this meekness when we are corrected by our Superiors or friends. St. Francis de Sales again writes: "To receive a reprimand willingly, shows that we love the virtue opposed to the fault for which we are corrected; and consequently this is a great sign of progress in perfection."2

We must besides practice meekness towards ourselves. It is a delusion of the devil, to make us consider it a virtue to be angry with ourselves for committing some fault; far from it, it is a trick of the enemy to keep us in a state of trouble, that so we may be unfit for the performance of any good. St. Francis de Sales said: "Hold for certain that all such thoughts as create disquiet are not from God, who is the Prince of peace, but proceed either from the devil, or from self-love, or from the good opinion we have of ourselves. These are the three sources from which all our troubles spring. When,

1 "Irascimini, et nolite peccare." Ps. 4.5.
2 *Spirit of St Francis de Sales*, ch. 19.

[399] therefore, any thoughts arise which throw us into trouble, we must immediately reject and despise them."1

Meekness is also more especially necessary when we have to correct others. Corrections made with a bitter zeal often do more harm than good, especially when he who must be corrected is himself excited: in such cases the correction should be put off, and we must wait until he is cool. And we ourselves ought no less to refrain from correcting while we are under the influence of ill-temper; for then our admonition will always be accompanied with harshness; and the person in fault, when he sees that he is corrected in such a way, will take no heed of the admonition, considering it the mere effect of passion. This holds good as far as concerns the good of our neighbor; as concerns our personal advantage, let us show how dearly we love Jesus Christ, by patiently and gladly supporting every sort of ill-treatment, injury, and contempt.

Affections and Prayers

O my despised Jesus, O love, O joy of my soul, You have by Your example made contempt most acceptable to Your lovers! I promise You, from this day forward, to submit to every insult for the love of You, who for love of me did submit on earth to every species of revilement from men. Do You grant me strength to keep this promise. Enable me to know and to perform whatever You desire at my hands. My God and my all, I crave no other good than Yourself, who are infinite good! O You who take my interests so much too heart, grant that my only care may be to gratify You! Grant that all my thoughts may be occupied in avoiding whatever may offend You, and in promoting whatever may contribute to Your good pleasure. Ward off every occasion that may draw me from Your love. I strip my self of my liberty, and consecrate it entirely to Your good will. I love You, O infinite goodness! I love You, O my delight! O Word incarnate, I love You more than myself! Take

1 *Letter* 51.

[400] pity on me, and heal whatever wounds remain in my poor

soul from its past disloyalties towards You. I resign myself wholly into Your arms, O my Jesus; I will be wholly Your; I will suffer every thing for love of You; and I ask of You nothing but Your self!

O Holy Virgin and my Mother Mary, I love you, and I rely on you; help me by your powerful intercession!

CHAPTER 9

LOVE THINKS NO EVIL, REJOICES NOT IN WHAT IS WRONG, BUT REJOICES WITH THE TRUTH
(Conformity To God's Will)

(Charitas non cogitat malum , non gaudet super iniquitate, congaudet autem veritati)

He that loves Jesus Christ only wishes what Jesus Christ wishes

LOVE and truth always go together; so that love, conscious that God is the only and the true good, detests iniquity, which is directly opposed to the divine will, and takes no satisfaction but in what pleases Almighty God. Hence the soul that loves God is heedless of what people say of it, and only aims at pleasing God. The Blessed Henry Suso said: "That man stands well with God who strives to conform himself to the truth, and for the rest is utterly indifferent to the opinion or treatment of man kind."

As we have already more than once asserted, the sanctity and perfection of a soul consists in renouncement of self and in submission to the will of God; but now it will be well to enter more into detail.

1. The Necessity of Conforming to the Will of God

If, then, we would become saints, our whole endeavor must be, never to follow our own will, but always the [401] will of God; the substance of all the precepts and divine counsels is comprised in doing and suffering what God wills, and in the manner he wills it. Let us, therefore, entreat the Lord to bestow on us a holy liberty of spirit;

liberty of spirit leads us to embrace whatever is pleasing to Jesus Christ, regardless of all feelings of repugnance arising from self-love and human respect. The love of Jesus Christ makes those who love him utterly indifferent; so that all things are alike to them, whether bitter or sweet: they do not wish for anything that pleases themselves, but only for that which is pleasing to God; they employ themselves in little and great things, be they pleasant or unpleasant, with the same peace of mind; it is enough for them if they please God.

St. Augustine says: "Love, and do what you like."[1] Whoever really loves God seeks only to please him; and in this is all his pleasure. St. Teresa says: "He that seeks but the gratification of one he loves, is gratified with all that pleases that person. Love in its perfection produces this result; it makes a person heedless of all private interests and self-satisfaction, and concentrates all his thoughts on endeavoring to please the person be loved, and to do all he can to honor him himself, and to make him honored by others. O Lord, all our ills come from not keeping our eyes fixed on You! Were we solely intent on advancing, we should soon come to the end of our journey; but we fall and stumble a thousand times, and we even lose our way, for not looking attentively to the right path." Here we may see what should be the single aim of all our thoughts, actions, desires, and of all our prayers, namely, the pleasure of God; our way to perfection must be this, to walk according to the will of God.

God wishes us to love him with our whole heart:

1 "Ama, et fac quod vis."

[402] *You shall love the Lord your God with your whole heart.*1 That person loves Jesus Christ with his whole heart who says to him with the Apostle: *Lord, what will You have me to do?*2 Lord, signify to me what You will have me do; for I desire to perform all. And let us be persuaded that while we desire what God desires, we desire what is best for ourselves; for assuredly God only wishes what is best for us. St. Vincent de Paul said: "Conformity with the will of God is the treasure of a Christian and the remedy for all evils; since it comprises abnegation of self and union with God and all virtues." In this, then, is all perfection: Lord, what will You have me to do? Jesus Christ promises us, *not a hair of your head shall perish.*3 Which is as much as to say, that the Lord rewards us for every good thought we have of pleasing him, and for every tribulation embraced with patience in conformity to his holy will. St. Teresa said, "The Lord never sends a trial, without remunerating it with some favor as often as we accept it with resignation."4

But our conformity to the divine will must be entire, without any reserve, and constant without withdrawal. In this consists the height of perfection; and to this (I repeat) all our works, all our desires, and all our prayers ought to tend. Some souls given to prayer, on reading of the ecstasies and raptures of St. Teresa and St. Philip Neri, come to wish to enjoy themselves these supernatural unions. Such wishes must be banished as contrary to humility; if we really desire to be saints, we must aspire after true union with God, which is to unite our will entirely to the will of God. St. Teresa 5 said:

1 "Diliges Dominum Deumtuum ex toto corde tuo." Matt. 22.37.
2 "Domine, quid me vis facere?" Acts 9.6.

3 "Et capillus de capite vestro non peribit." Luke 21.18.
4 *Life*, ch. 30.
5 *Foundations*, ch. 5.

[403] "Those persons are deceived who fancy that union
with God consists in ecstasies, raptures, and sensible enjoyments of him. It consists in nothing else than in submitting our will to the will of God; and this submission
is perfect when our will is detached from everything,
and so completely united with that of God, that all its
movements depend solely on the will of God. This is
the real and essential union which I have always sought
after, and continually beg of the Lord." And then she
adds: u Oh, how many of us say this, and seem to our
selves to desire nothing besides this; but, miserable
creatures that we are, how few of us attain to it!" Such,
indeed, is the undeniable truth; many of us say: O Lord!
I give You my will, I desire nothing but what You
desire; but, in the event of some trying occurrence,
we are at a loss how to yield calmly to the divine will.
And this is the source of our continually complaining
that we are unfortunate in the world, and that we are
the butt of every misfortune; and so of our dragging on
an unhappy life.

If we were conformed to the divine will in every
trouble, we should undoubtedly become saints, and be
the happiest of mankind. This, then, should form the
chief object of our attention, to keep our will in un
broken union with the will of God in every occurrence
of life, be it pleasant or unpleasant. It is the admonition of the Holy Spirit. *Winnow not with every wind.*1
Some people resemble the weathercocks, which turn
about every wind that blows; if the wind is fair and
favorable to their desires, they are all gladness and con-

descension; but if there blow a contrary wind, and things fall out against their desires, they are all sadness and impatience; this is why they do not become saints, and why their life is unhappy, because, in the present

1 "Ne ventiles te in omnem ventura." Ecclus. (Sirach) 5.11.

[404] life, adversity will always befall us in a greater measure than prosperity. St. Dorotheus said, that to receive from the hands of God whatever happens is a great means to keep ourselves in continual peace and tranquillity of soul. And the saint relates, that on this account the ancient Fathers of the desert were never seen angry or melancholy, because they accepted whatever happened to them joyfully, as coming from the hands of God. Oh, happy the man who lives wholly united and abandoned to the divine will! he is neither puffed up by success nor depressed by reverses; for he well knows that all alike comes from the self-same hand of God; the will of God is the single rule of his own will; thus he only does what God wishes him to do, and he only desires what God does. He is not anxious to do many things, but to accomplish with perfection what he knows to be acceptable to God. Accordingly, he prefers the minutest obligations of his state of life to the most glorious and important actions, well aware that in the latter self-love may find a great share, whereas in the former there is certainly the will of God.

Thus we, too, shall be happy when we receive from God all the dispositions of his Providence in the spirit of perfect conformity to his divine will, utterly regardless whether or not they coincide with our private inclinations. The saintly Mother de Chantal said: "When shall we come to relish the divine will in every event that happens, without paying attention to anything else but the good pleasure of God, from whom it is certain that prosperity and adversity proceed alike from motives of love and for our best interests? When shall we resign ourselves unreservedly into the arms of our most loving heavenly Father, entrusting him with the care of our persons and our affairs, and reserving nothing for ourselves but the sole desire of pleasing God?" The friends of St. Vincent de Paul said of him while he was still on [405] earth: "Vincent is always Vincent." By which they meant to say, that the saint was ever to be seen with the same smiling face, whether in prosperity or in adversity; and was always himself, because, as he lived in the total abandonment of himself to God, he feared nothing and desired nothing but what was pleasing to God. St. Teresa said: "By this holy abandonment that admirable liberty of spirit is generated, which those who are perfect possess, wherein they find all the happiness in this life which they can possibly desire; inasmuch as, fearful of nothing, and desirous or wanting for nothing in the things of this world, they possess all."1

Many, on the other hand, fabricate a sort of sanctity according to their own inclinations; some, inclined to melancholy, make sanctity consist in living in seclusion; others, of a busy temperament, in preaching and in making up quarrels; some, of an austere nature, in penitential inflictions and macerations; others, who are naturally generous, in distributing alms; some in saying many vocal prayers; others in visiting sanctuaries; and all their sanctity consists in such or the like practices. External acts are the fruit of the love of Jesus Christ; but true love itself consists in a complete conformity to the will of God; and as a consequence of this, in denying ourselves and in preferring what is most pleasing to

God, and solely because he deserves it.

Others wish to serve God; but it must be in that employment, in that place, with those companions, and in
such circumstances; or else they either neglect their
duty, or at least do it with a bad grace: such as these
are not free in spirit, but are slaves of self-love, and on
that account reap little merit even from what they per
form; moreover, they live in perpetual disquiet, since
their attachment to self-will makes the yoke of Jesus

1 *Foundations*, ch. 5.

[406] Christ become heavy to them. The true lovers of
Jesus Christ love only that which is pleasing to Jesus Christ,
and for the sole reason that it does please him; and they
love it when it pleases Jesus Christ, where it pleases him,
and how it pleases him; whether he chooses to employ
them in honorable functions, or in mean and lowly occu-
pations; in a life of notoriety in the world, or in one
hidden and despised. This is the real drift of what is
meant by the pure love of Jesus Christ; hence we must
labor to overcome the cravings of our self-love, which
seeks to be employed in those works only that are glorious, or that are according to our own inclinations. And
what will it profit us to be the most honored, the most
wealthy, the greatest in this world, without the will of
God? The Blessed Henry Suso said, "I would rather
be the vilest insect on earth by the will of God, than a
seraph in heaven by my own will."

Jesus Christ said: Many shall say: Lord, we have cast out
devils and done great wonders in Your name: *Lord, have
we not prophesied in Your name, and cast out devils in
Your name, and done many miracles in Your name?*1 But

the Lord will answer them: *I never knew you; depart from Me, you that work iniquity.*2 Depart from me; I never acknowledged you for my disciples, because you preferred to follow your own inclinations rather than my will. And this is especially applicable to those priests who labor much for the salvation or perfection of others, while they themselves continue to live on in the mire of their imperfections. Perfection consists: First, in a true contempt of one's self. Secondly, in a thorough mortification of our own appetites. Thirdly, in a perfect conformity to the will

1 "Domine, nonne in nomine tuo prophetavimus, et in nomine tuo daemonia ejecimus, et in nomine tuo virtutes multas fecimus?" Matt. 7.22.
2 "Nunquam novi vos; discedite a me, qui operamini iniquitatem." Matt. 7.23.

[407] of God: whosoever is wanting in one of these virtues is out of the way of perfection. On this account a great servant of God said, it was better for us in our actions to have the will of God rather than his glory as their sole end; for in doing the will of God, we at the same time promote his glory; whereas in proposing to ourselves the glory of God, we frequently deceive ourselves, and follow our own will under pretext of glorifying God. St. Francis de Sales said: "There are many who say to the Lord: I give myself wholly to You without reserve; but few indeed, in point of fact, practically embrace this abandonment. It consists in a certain indifference in accepting all kinds of events, just as they fall out according to the order of divine Providence, afflictions as well as consolations, slights and injuries as well as honor and glory."1

It is therefore in suffering, and in embracing with

cheerfulness whatever cuts against the grain of our own inclinations, that we can discover who is a true lover of Jesus Christ. Thomas a Kempis says "that he is not deserving of the name of lover who is not ready to endure all things for his beloved, and to follow in all things the will of his beloved."2 On the contrary, Father Balthazar Alvarez said, that whoever quietly resigns himself to the divine will in troubles "travels to God post-haste." And the saintly Mother Teresa said: "What greater acquisition can we make, than to have some proof that we are pleasing God?" And to this I add, that we cannot have a more certain proof of this, than by peacefully embracing the crosses which God sends us. We please God by thanking him for his benefits on earth; but, says Father John of Avila, one "blessed be God "uttered in adversity is worth six thousand acts of thanksgiving in prosperity.

1 *Entret.*, 2.
2 "Qui non est paratus omnia pati et ad voluntatem stare dilecti, non est dignus amator appellari." *Imitation of Christ*, Bk. 3, ch. 5.

[408] And here we must observe, that we must receive with resignation not merely the crosses which come directly from God; for instance, ill-health, scanty talents, accidental reverses of fortune; but such, moreover, as come indirectly from God, and directly from our fellow-men; for instance, persecutions, thefts, injuries; for all, in reality, come from God. David was one day insulted by one of his vassals called Shemei, who not only upbraided him with words of insult, but even threw stones at him. One of the courtiers would have immediately avenged the insult by cutting off the head of the offender; but David replied: *Let him alone, and let him curse; for the Lord has bid him curse David;*1 or, in other words, God

makes use of him to chastise me for my sins, and therefore he allowed him to pursue me with injuries.

Thus St. Mary Magdalene de Pazzi said that all
our prayers should have for their end to obtain from
God the grace to follow his holy will in all things. Certain souls; greedy of spiritual dainties in prayer, go in
search only of these banquets of sweet and tender feelings; but courageous souls that seek sincerely to belong
wholly to God, ask him only for light to understand his
will, and for strength to put it in execution. In order to
attain to purity of love, it is necessary to submit our will
in all things to the will of God: "Never consider your
selves," said St. Francis de Sales, "to have arrived at
the purity which you ought to have, as long as your will
is not cheerfully obedient, even in things the most re-
pulsive, to the will of God." "Because," as St. Teresa
remarks, "the giving up of our will to God draws him
to unite himself to our lowliness." 2 But this can never
be obtained, except by means of mental prayer and of
continual petitions addressed to the divine majesty, nor

1 "Dimitte eum ut maledicat; Dominus enim precepit ei ut male-
diceret David." 2 Kings, 16.10.
2 *Way of Perfection*, ch. 33.

[409] without a cordial desire to belong entirely to Jesus
Christ without reserve.

Most amiable Heart of my divine Savior, Heart
enamored of mankind, since You love us with such
a depth of tenderness; O Heart, therefore, worthy to rule
over and possess all our hearts, would that I could make
all men comprehend the love You have for them, and
the tender caresses You do lavish on those who love

You without reserve! O Jesus my love, be pleased to accept the offering and the sacrifice which I this day make to You of my entire will! Acquaint me with what You would have me to do; for I am determined to do all by the help of Your grace.

2. Obedience

Now what is the surest way to know and ascertain what God requires of us? There is no surer way than to practice obedience to our Superiors and directors. St. Vincent de Paul said: " The will of God is never better complied with than when we obey our Superiors." The Holy Spirit says: *Much better is obedience than the victims of fools.*1 God is more pleased with the sacrifice which we make to him of our own will, by submitting it to obedience, than with all other sacrifices which we can offer him; because in other things, as in alms-deeds, fastings, mortifications, and the like, we give of what is ours to God, but in giving him our will we present him ourselves: when we give him our goods, our mortifications, we give him part; but when we give him our will, we give him everything. So that when we say to God, O Lord, make me know by means of obedience what You require of me, for I wish to comply with all, we have nothing more to offer him.

1 "Melior est obedientia, quam stultorum victimae." Eccles. 4.17.

[410] Whoever, therefore, gives himself up to obedience, must needs detach himself totally from his own opinion. " What though each one," says St. Francis de Sales, "has his own opinions, virtue is not thereby violated; but virtue is violated by the attachment which we have to our own opinions."1 But alas! this attachment is the

hardest thing to part with; and hence there are so few persons wholly given to God, because few render a thorough submission to obedience. There are some persons so fondly attached to their own opinion, that, on receiving an obedience, although the thing enjoined suit their inclination, yet, from the very fact that it is commanded, they lose all fancy for it, all wish to discharge it; for they find no relish in anything but in following the dictates of their individual will. How different is the conduct of saints! their only happiness flows from the execution of what obedience imposes on them. The saintly Mother Jane Frances de Chantal once told her daughters that they might spend the recreation-day in any manner they chose. When the evening came, they all went to her, to beg most earnestly that she would never again grant them such a permission; for they had never spent such a wearisome day as that on which they had been set free from obedience.

It is a delusion to think that any one can be possibly better employed than in the discharge of what obedience has imposed. St. Francis de Sales says: "To desert an occupation given by obedience in order to unite ourselves to God by prayer, by reading, or by recollection, would be to withdraw from God to unite ourselves to our own self-love."2 St. Teresa adds, moreover, that whoever performs any work, even though it be spiritual, yet against obedience, assuredly works by the instigation of the devil, and not by divine inspiration, as he perhaps

1 *Entret.* 14.
2 *Spirit of St Francis de Sales,* ch. 19.

[411] flatters himself; "because," says the saint, "the inspirations of God always come in company with obedience."

To the same effect she says elsewhere; "God requires nothing more of a soul that is determined to love him than obedience."1 "A work done out of obedience," says Father Rodriguez, "outweighs every other that we can imagine." To lift up a straw from the ground out of obedience is of greater merit than a protracted prayer, or a discipline to blood, through our own will. This caused St. Mary Magdalene de Pazzi to say, that she would rather be engaged in some exercise from obedience than in prayer; "because," said she, "in obedience I am certain of the will of God, whereas I am by no means so certain of it in any other exercise."2 According to all spiritual masters, it is better to leave off any devout exercise through obedience, than to continue it without obedience. The Most Blessed Virgin Mary revealed once to St. Bridget,3 that he who relinquishes some mortification through obedience reaps a twofold profit; since he has already obtained the merit of the mortification by the good-will to do it, and he also gains the merit of obedience by foregoing it. One day the famous Father Francis Arias went to see the Venerable Father John of Avila, his intimate friend, and he found him pensive and sad; he asked him the reason, and received this answer: "O happy you, who live under obedience, and are sure of doing the will of God. As for me, who shall assure me whether I do a thing more pleasing to God in going from village to village, catechizing the poor peasants, or in remaining stationary in the confessional, to hear every one that presents himself? Whereas he that is living under obedience is always sure that whatever he performs by obedience is according to the will of God, or rather that it is what is most acceptable to God." Let

1 *Foundations*, ch. 5.
2 *Cepar.* ch. 5.

3 *Rev.* Bk. 4, ch. 26.

[412] this serve as a consolation for all those who live under obedience.

For obedience to be perfect, we must obey with the will and with the judgment. To obey with the will signifies to obey willingly, and not by constraint, after the fashion of slaves; to obey with the judgment means to conform our judgment to that of the Superior, without examining what is commanded. St. Mary Magdalene de Pazzi remarks on this: "Perfect obedience demands a soul without judgment." To the like purpose, St. Philip Neri said that, in order to obey with perfection, it was not enough to execute the thing commanded, but it must be done without reasoning on it; taking it for certain that what is commanded us is for us the most perfect thing we can do, although the opposite might be better before God.1

This holds good not merely for religious, but likewise for seculars living under obedience to their spiritual directors. Let them request their director to prescribe them rules for the guidance of their affairs, both spiritual and temporal; and so they will make sure of doing what is best. St. Philip Neri said: "Let those who are desirous of progressing in the way of God submit themselves to a prudent confessor, whom they should obey as in God's place. By so doing, we are certain of not having to render an account to God of the actions we perform."2

He said, moreover, "that we must place faith in the confessor, because the Lord will not permit him to err; that nothing is so sure of cutting off all the snares of the devil as to do the will of others in the performance of good; and that there is nothing more dangerous than to wish to direct ourselves according to our private fancy." In like manner, St. Francis de Sales says, in speaking of the direction of the spiritual Father as a means of walk-

1 *Bacci*, Bk. 1, ch. 20.
2 *Ibid.*

[413] ing securely in the path of perfection, "This is the maxim of all maxims."1 "Seek as you will," says the devout Avila, "you will never so surely find the will of God as in the way of this humble obedience, so much recommended and so practiced by all the ancient servants of God." The same thing is affirmed by St. Bernard, St. Bernardine of Siena, St. Antoninus, St. John of the Cross, St. Teresa, John Gerson, and all theologians and masters of the spiritual life; and St. John of the Cross said, that to call this truth in question is almost to doubt of the faith. The words of the saint are, "not to be sat isfied with what the confessor says, is arrogance, and a lack of faith."

Among the maxims of St. Francis de Sales are the two following, most consolatory for scrupulous souls: "First, a truly obedient soul was never yet lost; secondly, we ought to be satisfied on being told by our spiritual director that we are going on well, without seeking to be convinced of it ourselves." It is the teaching of many Doctors, as of Gerson, St. Antoninus, Cajetanus, Navarrus, Sanchez, Bonacina, Cordovius, Castropalao, and the Doctors of Salamanca, with others, that the scrupulous person is bound, under strict obligation, to act in opposition to scruples, when from such scruples there is reason to apprehend grievous harm happening to soul or body, such as the loss of health, or of intellect;

wherefore scrupulous persons ought to have greater scruple at not obeying the confessor than at acting in opposition to their scruples.

To sum up, therefore, all that has been said in this chapter, our salvation and perfection consist: 1. In denying ourselves; 2. In following the will of God; 3. In praying him always to give us strength to do both one and the other.

1 *Introduction to the Devout Life,* Pt. 1, ch. 4.

Affections and Prayers

[414] *What have I in heaven? and besides You what do I desire upon earth? You are the God of my heart, and the God that is my portion forever.* 1 My beloved Redeemer, infinitely amiable, since You have come down from heaven to give Yourself wholly to me, what else shall I seek for on earth or in heaven besides You, who are the sovereign good, the only good worthy to be loved? Be You, then, the sole Lord of my heart, do You possess it entirely: may my soul love You alone, obey You alone, and seek to please no other than You. Let others enjoy the riches of this world, I wish only for You: You are and shall ever be my treasure in this life and in eternity Wherefore I give You, O my Jesus, my whole heart and all my will. It was at one time, alas! a rebel against You; but now I dedicate it wholly to You. *Lord, what will You have me to do?*2 Tell me what You require of me, and lend me Your assistance; for I will leave nothing undone. Dispose of me, and of all that concerns me, as You please; I accept of all, and resign myself to all. O Love deserving of infinite love, You have loved me so as even to die for me; I love You with my whole heart, I love You more than myself, and into Your hands I abandon my soul. On this very day I bid farewell to every worldly affection, I take leave of everything created, and

I give myself without reserve to You; Through the merits of Your Passion receive me, and make me faithful unto death. My Jesus, my Jesus, from this day forward I will live only for You, I will love none but You, I will seek nothing else than to do Your blessed will.

Aid me by Your grace, and aid me, too, by your protection, O Mary my hope.

1 "Quid mihi est in coelo? et a te quid volui super terram? . . . Deus cordis mei, et pars mea, Deus, in aeternum." Ps. 72.25.
2 "Domine quid me vis facere?" Acts, 9.6.

CHAPTER X

LOVE BEARS ALL THINGS
(Fortitude)
(Charitas omnia suffert)

He that loves Jesus Christ bears all Things for Jesus Christ, and especially Illnesses, Poverty, and Contempt.

[415] IN Chapter 1 we spoke of the virtue of patience in general. In this we will speak of certain matters in particular, which demand the especial practice of patience.

Father Balthazar Alvarez 1 said that a Christian need not imagine himself to have made any progress until he has succeeded in penetrating his heart with a lasting sense of the sorrows, poverty, and disgraces of Jesus Christ so as to support with loving patience every sort of sorrow, privation, and contempt, for the sake of Jesus Christ.

1. Patience in Sickness

In the first place, let us speak of bodily infirmities which, when borne with patience, merit for us a beautiful crown.

St. Vincent de Paul said: "Did we but know how precious a treasure is contained in infirmities, we should accept of them with joy as the greatest possible blessings." Hence the saint himself, though constantly afflicted with ailments, that often left him no rest day or night, bore them with so much peace and such serenity of countenance that no one could guess that anything ailed him at all. Oh, how edifying is it to see a sick person bear

[416] his illness with a peaceful countenance, as did St.
Francis de Sales! When he was ill, he simply explained his
complaint to the physician, obeyed him exactly by taking the prescribed medicines, however nauseous; and
for the rest he remained at peace, never uttering a single
complaint in all his sufferings. What a contrast to this
is the conduct of those who do nothing but complain
even for the most trifling indisposition, and who would
like to have around them all their relatives and friends
to sympathize with them! Far different was the in-
struction of St. Teresa to her nuns: "My sisters, learn
to suffer something for the love of Jesus Christ, without
letting all the world know of it."1 One Good Friday
Jesus Christ favored the Venerable Father Louis da
Ponte with so much bodily suffering, that no part of him
was exempt from its particular pain: he mentioned his
severe sufferings to a friend; but he was afterwards so
sorry at having done so, that he made a vow never again
to reveal to anybody whatever he might afterwards
suffer. I say "he was favored;" for, to the saints, the
illnesses and pains which God sends them are real
favors. One day St. Francis of Assisi lay on his bed in
excruciating torments; a companion said to him: "Father, beg God to ease your pains, and not to lay so
heavy a hand upon you." On hearing this, the saint
instantly leaped from his bed, and going on his knees,
thanked God for his sufferings; then, turning to his
companion, he said: "Listen, did I not know that you
so spoke from simplicity, I would refuse ever to see you
again."2

Some one that is sick will say, it is not so much the

infirmity itself that afflicts me, as that it disables me from going to church to perform my devotions, to communicate, and to hear Holy Mass; I cannot go to choir

1 *Way of Perfection*, ch. 12.
2 *Life*, ch. 14.

[417] to recite the divine Office with my brethren; I cannot celebrate Mass; I cannot pray; for my head is aching with pain, and is light almost to fainting. But tell me now, if you please, why do you wish to go to church or to choir? why would you communicate and say or hear Holy Mass? is it to please God? but it is not now the pleasure of God that you say the Office, that you communicate, or hear Mass; but that you remain patiently on this bed, and support the pains of this infirmity. But you are displeased with my speaking thus; then you are not seeking to do what is pleasing to God, but what is pleasing to yourself. The Venerable John of Avila wrote as follows to a priest who so complained to him: "My friend, busy not yourself with what you would do if you were well, but be content to remain ill as long as God thinks fit. If you seek the will of God, what matters it to you whether you be well or ill?"1

You say you are unable even to pray, because your head is weak. Be it so: you cannot meditate; but why cannot you make acts of resignation to the will of God? If you would only make these acts, you could not make a better prayer, welcoming with love all the torments that assail you. So did St. Vincent de Paul: when attacked by a serious illness, he was accustomed to keep himself tranquilly in the presence of God, without forcing his mind to dwell on any particular subject; his sole exercise was to elicit some short acts from time to time, as of love, of confidence, of thanksgiving, and more frequently of resignation, especially in the crisis of his sufferings. St. Francis de Sales made this remark: "Considered in themselves, tribulations are terrifying; but considered in the will of God, they are lovely and delightful."2 You cannot say prayers; and what more exquisite prayer than to cast a look from time to time

1 Part 2, Letter 54.
2 *Love of God*, Bk. 9, ch. 2.

[418] on your crucified Lord, and to offer him your pains, uniting the little that you endure to the overwhelming torments that afflicted Jesus on the cross!

There was a certain pious lady lying bedridden with many disorders; and on the servant putting the crucifix into her hand, and telling her to pray to God to deliver her from her miseries, she made answer: "But how can you desire me to seek to descend from the cross, while I hold in my hand a God crucified? God forbid chat I should do so. I will suffer for him who chose to suffer torments for me incomparably greater than mine."1 This was, indeed, precisely what Jesus Christ said to St. Teresa when she was laboring under serious illness; he appeared to her all covered with wounds, and then said to her: "Behold, my daughter, the bitterness of my suf - ferings, and consider if yours equal mine." Hence the saint was accustomed to say, in the midst of her infirmities: "When I remember in how many ways my Savior suffered, though he was innocence itself, I know not how it could enter my head to complain of my suf - ferings." During a period of thirty-eight years, St. Lidwine was afflicted with numberless evils fevers, gout in the feet and hands, and sores, all her lifetime; never theless, from never losing sight of the sufferings of Jesus Christ, she maintained an unbroken cheerfulness and joy. In like manner, St. Joseph of Leonessa, a Capuchin, when the surgeon was about to amputate his arm, and his brethren would have bound him, to prevent him from stirring through vehemence of pain, seized hold of the crucifix and exclaimed: "Why do you bind me? Why do you bind me? behold who it is that binds me to support every suffering patiently for love of him;" and so he bore the operation without a murmur. St. Jonas the Martyr, after passing the entire night immersed in ice by order

1 *Life*, additions.

[419] of the tyrant, declared next morning that he had never spent a happier night, because he had pictured to him self Jesus hanging on the cross; and thus, compared with the torments of Jesus, his own had seemed rather caresses than torments.

Oh, what abundance of merits may be accumulated by patiently enduring illnesses! Almighty God revealed to Father Balthazar Alvarez the great glory he had in store for a certain nun, who had borne a painful sickness with resignation; and told him that she had acquired greater merit in those eight months of her illness than some other religious in many years. It is by the patient endurance of ill-health that we weave a great part, and perhaps the greater part, of the crown that God destines for us in heaven. St. Lidwine had a revelation to this effect. After sustaining many and most cruel disorders, as we mentioned above, she prayed to die a martyr for the love of Jesus Christ; now as she was one day sighing after this martyrdom, she suddenly saw a beautiful crown, but still incomplete, and she understood that it was destined for herself; whereupon the saint, longing to behold it completed, entreated the Lord to increase her sufferings. Her prayer was heard, for some soldiers came shortly after, and ill-treated her, not only with injurious words, but with blows and outrages. An angel then appeared to her with the crown completed, and informed her that those last injuries had added to it the gems that were wanting; and shortly afterwards she expired.

Ah, yes! to the hearts that fervently love Jesus Christ, pains and disgraces are most delightful. And thus we see the holy martyrs going with gladness to encounter the sharp prongs and hooks of iron, the plates of glowing steel and axes. The martyr St. Procopius thus spoke to the tyrant who tortured him: "Torment me as you like; but know at the same time, that nothing is sweeter [420] to the lover of Jesus Christ than to suffer for his sake."1

St. Gordius, Martyr, replied in the same way to the tyrant who threatened him death: "You threaten me with death; but I am only sorry that I cannot die more than once for my own beloved Jesus."2 And I ask. did these saints speak thus because they were insensible to pain or weak in intellect? "No," replies St. Bernard; "not insensibility, but love caused this."3 They were not insensible, for they felt well enough the torments in-flicted on them; but since they loved God, they esteemed it a great privilege to suffer for God, and to lose all, even life itself, for the love of God.

Above all, in time of sickness we should be ready to accept of death, and of that death which God pleases. We must die, and our life must finish in our last illness;

nor do we know which will be our last illness. Where fore in every illness we must be prepared to accept that death which God has appointed for us. A sick person says: "Yes; but I have committed many sins, and have done no penance. I should like to live, not for the sake of living, but to make some satisfaction to God before my death." But tell me, my brother, how do you know that if you live longer you will do penance, and not rather do worse than before? At present you can well cherish the hope that God has pardoned you; what penance can be more satisfactory than to accept of death with resignation, if God so wills it? St. Aloysius Gonzaga, at the age of twenty-three, gladly embraced death with this reflection: "At present," he said, "I am, as I hope, in the grace of God. Hereafter, I know not what may befall me; so that I now die contentedly, if God calls me to the next life."4 It was the opinion of Father

1 *Ap. Sur.*, 8 Jul.
2 *S. Bas. hom, in Gord. M.*
3 "Neque hoc facit stupor, sed amor." *On the Song of Songs*, sermon 61.
4 *Life*, ch. 25.

[421] John of Avila that every one, provided he be in good dispositions, though only moderately good, should desire death, to escape the danger, which always surrounds us in this world, of possibly sinning and losing the grace of God.

Besides, owing to our natural frailty, we cannot live in this world without committing at least venial sins; this should be a motive for us to embrace death willingly, that we may never offend God any more. Further, if we truly love God, we should ardently long to go to see him, and love him with all our strength in Paradise, which no one can do perfectly in this present life; but unless death open us the door, we cannot enter that blessed region of love. This caused St. Augustine, that loving soul, to cry out: "Oh, let me die, Lord, that I may behold You!" 1 O Lord, let me die, otherwise I cannot behold and love You face to face.

2. Patience in Poverty

In the second place, we must practice patience in the endurance of poverty. Our patience is certainly very much tried when we are in need of temporal goods. St. Augustine said: "He that has not God, has nothing; he that has God, has all."2 He who possesses God, and remains united to his blessed will, finds every good. Witness St. Francis, barefooted, clad in sackcloth, and deprived of all things, yet happier than all the monarchs of the world, by simply repeating, "My God and my all."3 A poor man is properly he that has not what he desires; but he that desires nothing, and is contented with his poverty, is in fact very rich. Of such St. Paul

1 "Eia, Domine! moriar, ut te videam." *Sol. an. ad Dom.* ch. 1.
2 Sermon 85.
3 "Deus meus, et omnia."

[422] says: *Having nothing, yet possessing all things.*1 The true lovers of God have nothing, and yet have every-thing; since, when temporal goods fail them, they exclaim: "My Jesus, You alone are sufficient for me;" and with this they rest satisfied. Not only did the saints main-tain patience in poverty, but sought to be despoiled of all, in order to live detached from all, and united with God alone. If we have not courage enough to renounce

all worldly goods, at all events let us be contented with
that state of life in which God has placed us; let our
solicitude be not for earthly goods, but for those of
Paradise, which are immeasurably greater, and last forever; and let us be fully persuaded of what St. Teresa
says: "The less we have here, the more we shall have
there."2

St. Bonaventure said that temporal goods were nothing
more than a sort of bird-lime to hinder the soul from
flying to God. And St. John Climacus 3 said, that poverty, on the contrary, is a path which leads to God free
of all hindrances. Our Lord himself said: *Blessed are
the poor in spirit, for theirs is the kingdom of heaven.*4 In
the other Beatitudes, the heaven of the life to come is promised to the meek and to the clean of heart; but to the
poor, heaven (that is, heavenly joy) is promised even in
this life: theirs is the kingdom of heaven. Yes, for even in
the present life the poor enjoy a foretaste of paradise.
By the poor in spirit are meant those who are not merely
poor in earthly goods, but who do not so much as desire
them; who, having enough to clothe and feed them, live
contented, according to the advice of the Apostle: *But
having food, and with which to be covered, with these we*

1 "Nihil habentes, et omnia possidentes." 2 Cor. 6.10.
2 *Foundations*, ch. 14.
3 *Ladder of Divine Ascent*, 17.
4 "Beati pauperes spiritu, quoniam ipsorum est regnum coelorum."
Matt. 5.3.

[423] *are content.*1 Oh, blessed poverty (exclaimed St.
Laurence Justinian), which possesses nothing and fears
nothing; she is ever joyous and ever in abundance, since
she turns every inconvenience into advantage for the

soul.2 St. Bernard said: "The avaricious man hungers after earthly things as a beggar, the poor man despises them as a lord."3 The miser is always hungry as a beggar, because he is never satiated with the possessions he desires; the poor man, on the contrary, despises them all as a rich lord, inasmuch as he desires nothing.

One day Jesus Christ thus spoke to the Blessed Angela of Foligno: "If poverty were not of great excellence, I would not have chosen it for myself, nor have bequeathed it to my elect." And, in fact, the saints, seeing Jesus poor, had therefore a great affection for poverty. St. Paul says that the desire of growing rich is a snare of Satan, by which he has wrought the ruin of innumerable souls: *They that will become rich, fall into temptation, and into the snare of the devil, and into many unprofitable and hurtful desires, which drown men into destruction and perdi-*
*tion.*4 Unhappy beings who, for the sake of vile creatures of earth, forfeit an infinite good, which is God! St. Basil the Martyr was quite in the right, when the Emperor Licinius proposed to make him the chief among his priests, if he would renounce Jesus Christ; he was right, I say, to reply: "Tell the emperor, that were he to give me his whole kingdom, he would not give me as much as he would rob me of, by depriving me of God."5

1 "Habentes autem alimenta et quibus tegamur, his contenti sumus." 1 Tim. 6.8.
2 *De Disch.* man. ch. 2.
3 "Avarus terrena esurit ut mendicus, fidelis contemnit ut dominus." *On the Song of Songs,* sermon 21.
4 "Qui volunt divites fieri, incidunt ... in laqueum diaboli et desideria . . . nociva, quae mergunt homines in interitum et perditionem. 1 Tim. 6.9.
5 *Boll.* April 26, Act. n. 11.

[424] Let us be content then with God, and with those things which he gives us, rejoicing in our poverty, when we stand in need of something we desire, and have it not; for herein consists our merit. "Not poverty," says St. Bernard, "but the love of poverty, is reckoned a virtue."1 Many are poor, but from not loving their poverty, they merit nothing; therefore St. Bernard says that the virtue of poverty consists not in being poor, but in the love of poverty,

This love of poverty should be especially practiced by religious who have made the vow of poverty. "Many religious," says the same St. Bernard, "wish to be poor; but on the condition of wanting for nothing."2 "Thus," says St. Francis de Sales, "they wish for the honor of poverty, but not the inconveniences of poverty."3 To such persons is applicable the saying of the Blessed Salomea, a nun of St. Clare: "That religious shall be a laughing-stock to angels and to men, who pretends to be poor, and yet murmurs when she is in need some-thing." Good religious act differently; they love their poverty above all riches. The daughter of the Emperor Maximilian II, a discalced nun of St. Clare, called Sister Margaret of the Cross, appeared on one occasion before her brother, the Archduke Albert, in a patched-up habit, who evinced some astonishment, as if it were unbecom -ing her noble birth; but she made him this answer: "My brother, I am more content with this torn garment than all monarchs with their purple robes." St. Mary Magdalene de Pazzi said: "O happy religious! who, detached from all by means of holy poverty, can say,

1 "Non paupertas virtus reputatur, sed paupertatis amor." *Epist.* 100.
2 "Pauperes esse volunt, eo tamen pacto, ut nihil eis desit." *In*

Adventu Domini, sermon 4.
3 *Introduction to the Devout Life*, ch. 16.

[425] *The Lord is the portion of my inheritance.*1 "My
God, You are my portion and all my good."2 St. Teresa,
having received a large alms from a certain merchant,
sent him word that his name was written in the Book of
Life, and that, in token of this, he should lose all his
possessions; and the merchant actually failed, and remained in poverty till death. St. Aloysius Gonzaga
said that there could be no surer sign that a person is
numbered among the elect, than to see him fearing God,
and at the same time undergoing crosses and tribulations
in this life.

The bereavement of relatives and friends by death be
longs also, in some measure, to holy poverty; and in this
we must especially practice patience. Some people, at
the loss of a parent or friend, can find no rest; they shut
themselves up to weep in their chamber, and giving free
vent to their sorrow, become insupportable to all around
them, by their lack of patience. I would ask these persons, for whose gratification they thus lament and shed
tears? For that of God? Certainly not; for God's will is,
that they should be resigned to his dispensations. For
that of the soul departed? By no means: if the soul be
lost, she abhors both you and your tears; if she be saved,
and already in heaven, she would have you thank God on
her part; if still in purgatory, she craves the help of your
prayers, and wishes you to bow with resignation to the
divine will, and to become a saint, in order that she may
one day enjoy your society in paradise. Of what use,
then, is all this weeping? On one occasion, the Venerable
Father Joseph Caracciolo, the Theatine, was surrounded
by his relatives, who were all bitterly lamenting the

death of his brother, whereupon he said to them:
"Come, come! let us keep these tears for a better purpose, to weep over the death of Jesus Christ, who has

1 "Dominus pars haereditatis meae." Ps. 15.5.
2 *Cepar.* ch. 22.

[426] been to us a father, a brother, and spouse, and who
died for love of us." On such occasions we must imitate
Job, who, on hearing the news of the death of his sons,
exclaimed, with full resignation to the Divine will, The
Lord gave, and the Lord has taken away God gave me
my sons, and God has taken them away. As it has pleased
the Lord, so is it done: *blessed be the name of the Lord;*1
it has pleased God that such things should happen, and so
it pleases me; wherefore may he be blessed by me forever.

3. Patience under Contempt

In the third place, we must practice patience, and show
our love to God, by tranquilly submitting to contempt.

As soon as a soul delivers herself up to God, he sends
her from himself, or through others, insults and persecution. One day an angel appeared to the Blessed
Henry Suso and said to him, "Henry, you have hitherto
mortified yourself in your own way; henceforth you shall
be mortified after the pleasure of others." On the day
following, as he was looking from a window on the street,
he saw a dog shaking and tearing a rag which it held
in its mouth; at the same moment a voice said to him,
"So have you to be torn in the mouths of men." Immediately the Blessed Henry descended into the street and
secured the rag, putting it by to encourage him in his
coming trials.2

Insults and injuries were the delicacies the saints
earnestly longed and sought for. St. Philip Neri, during the space of thirty years, had to put up with much

1 "Dominus dedit, Dominus abstulit: sicut Domino placuit,
ita factum est; sit nomen Domini benedictum." Job 1.21.
2 *Life*, ch. 22.

[427] ill-treatment in the house of St. Jerome at Rome; but
on this very account he refused to leave it, and resisted
all the invitations of his sons to come and live with them
in the new Oratory, founded by himself, till he received
an express command from the Pope to do so. So St.
John of the Cross was prescribed change of air for an
illness which eventually carried him to the grave; now,
he could have selected a more commodious convent, of
which the Prior was particularly attached to him; but
he chose instead a poor convent, whose Prior was his
enemy, and who, in fact, for a long time, and almost
up to his dying day, spoke ill of him, and abused him
in many ways, and even prohibited the other monks
from visiting him. Here we see how the saints even
sought to be despised. St. Teresa wrote this admirable maxim: "Whoever aspires to perfection must beware of ever saying: They had no reason to treat me so.
If you will not bear any cross but one which is founded
on reason, then perfection is not for you." While St.
Peter Martyr was complaining in prison of being con-
fined unjustly, he received that celebrated answer from
the Crucifix: our Lord said to him, *"And what evil have
I done, that I suffer and die on this cross for men?"* Oh,
what consolation do the saints derive in all their tribulations from the disgraces which Jesus Christ endured!
St. Eleazar, on being asked by his wife how he contrived

to bear with so much patience the many injuries which
he had to sustain, and that even from his own servants,
replied: "I turn my looks on the outraged Jesus, and
I discover immediately that my insults are a mere
nothing in comparison with what he suffered for my
sake; and thus God gives me strength to support all
patiently."

Therefore insults, poverty, torments, and all tribulations,
serve only to estrange further from God the soul that
does not love him; whereas, when they befall a soul in
[428] love with God, they become an instrument of
closer union and more ardent love of God: *Many waters
cannot quench love.*1 However great and grievous
troubles may be, so far from extinguishing the flames of
charity, they only serve to enkindle them the more in a
soul that loves nothing else but God.

But wherefore does Almighty God load us with so
many crosses, and take pleasure in seeing us afflicted,
reviled, persecuted, and ill-treated by the world? Is he,
by chance, a tyrant, whose cruel disposition makes him
rejoice in our suffering? No: God is by no means a
tyrant, nor cruel; he is all compassion and love towards
us; suffice it to say, that he has died for us. He indeed
does rejoice at our suffering, but for our good; inasmuch
as, by suffering here, we are released hereafter from the
debt of torments justly due from us to his divine justice;
he rejoices in them, because they detach us from the
sensual pleasures of this world: when a mother would
wean her child, she puts gall on the breast, in order to
create a disgust in the child; he rejoices in them, because
we give him, by our patience and resignation in bearing them, a token of our love; in short, he rejoices in
them, because they contribute to our increase of glory in

heaven. Such are the reasons for which the Almighty, in his compassion and love towards us, is pleased at our suffering.

Let us now draw this chapter to a conclusion. That we may be able to practice patience to advantage in all our tribulations, we must be fully persuaded that every trial comes from the hands of God, either directly, or in directly through men; we must therefore render God thanks whenever we are beset with sorrows, and accept, with gladness of heart, of every event, prosperous or adverse, that proceeds from him, knowing that all happens

1 "Aquae multae non potuerunt exstinguere charitatem." Song of Songs, 8.7.

[429] by his disposition for our welfare: *To them that love God,all things work together unto good.*1 In addition to this, it is well in our tribulations to glance a moment at that hell which we have formerly deserved: for assuredly all the pains of this life are incomparably smaller than the awful pains of hell. But above all, prayer, by which we gain the divine assistance, is the great means to suffer patiently all affliction, scorn, and contradictions; and is that which will furnish us with the strength which we have not of ourselves. The saints were persuaded of this; they recommended themselves to God, and so over came every kind of torments and persecutions.

Affections and Prayers

O Lord, I am fully persuaded that without suffering, and suffering with patience, I cannot win the crown of Paradise. David said: *From Him is my patience.*2 And I say the same; my patience in suffering must come from You. I make many purposes to accept in peace of all tribulations; but no sooner are they at hand than I grow sad and alarmed; and if I suffer, I suffer without merit and without love, because I know not how to suffer them so as to please You. O my Jesus, through the merits of Your patience in bearing so many afflictions for love of me, grant me the grace to bear crosses for the love of You! I love You with my whole heart, O my dear Redeemer! I love You, my sovereign good! I love You, my own love, worthy of infinite love. I am grieved at any displeasure I have ever caused You, more than for any evil whatever. I promise You to receive with patience all the trials You may send me; but I look to You for help to be faithful to my promise, and especially to be enabled to bear in peace the throes of my last agony and death.

Mary, my Queen, vouchsafe to obtain for me a true resignation in all the anguish and trials that await me in life and death.

1 "Diligentibus Deum omnia cooperantur in bonum." Rom. 8.28.
2 "Ab ipso patientia mea." Ps. 62.6.

CHAPTER 11

LOVE BELIEVES ALL THINGS
(Faith)
(*Charitas omnia credit*)

He that loves Jesus Christ believes all His Words

[430] WHOEVER loves a person, believes all that proceeds from the lips of that person; consequently, the more a soul loves Jesus Christ, the more lively and unshaken is her faith. When the good thief beheld our Redeemer, though he had done no ill, suffering death upon the cross with such patience, he began at once to love him; under the influence of this love, and of the divine light which then broke upon his soul, he believed that this was truly the Son of God, and begged not to be for gotten by him when he should have passed into his kingdom.

Faith is the foundation of love; but faith afterwards receives its perfection from love. His faith is most perfect whose love of God is most perfect. Charity produces in man not merely the faith of the understand ing, but the faith of the will also: those who believe only with the understanding, but not with the will, as is the case with sinners who are perfectly convinced of the truths of the faith, but do not choose to live according to the divine commandments, such as these have a very weak faith; for had they a more lively belief that the grace of God is a priceless treasure, and that sin, because it. robs us of this grace, is the worst of evils, they would assuredly change their lives. If, then, they prefer the miserable creatures of this earth to God, it is because they either do not believe, or because their faith is very

weak. On the contrary, he who believes not only with
[431] the understanding, but also with the will, so that he
not only believes, but has the will to believe in God, the re-
vealer of truth, from the love he has for him, and rejoices
in so believing, such a one has a perfect faith, and consequently seeks to make his life conformable to the truths
that he believes.

Weakness of faith, however, in those who live in sin,
does not spring from the obscurity of faith; for though
God, in order to make our faith more meritorious, has
veiled the objects of faith in darkness and secrecy, he
has at the same time given us so clear and convincing
evidence of their truth, that not to believe them would
argue not merely a lack of sense, but sheer madness and
impiety. The weakness of the faith of many persons is to
be traced to their wickedness of living. He who, rather
than forego the enjoyment of forbidden pleasures, scorns
the divine friendship, would wish there were no law to
forbid, and no chastisement to punish, his sin; on this account he strives to blind himself to the eternal truths of
death, judgment, and hell, and of divine justice; and because such subjects strike too much terror into his heart,
and are too apt to mix bitterness in his cup of pleasure, he
sets his brain to work to discover proofs, which have at
least the look of plausibility; and by which he allows
himself to be flattered into the persuasion that there is
no soul, no God, no hell, in order that he may live and
die like the brute beasts, without laws and without
reason.

And this laxity of morals is the source from which have
issued, and still issue daily, so many books and systems
of Materialists, Indifferentists, Utopians, Deists, and
Naturalists; some among them deny the divine exist-

ence, and some the divine Providence, saying that God, after having created men, takes no further notice of them, and is heedless whether they love or hate him whether they be saved or lost; others, again, deny the [432] goodness of God, and maintain that he has created numberless souls for hell, becoming himself their tempter to sin, that so they may damn themselves, and go into everlasting fire, to curse him there forever.

Oh, ingratitude and wickedness of men! God has created them in his mercy, to make them eternally happy in heaven; he has poured on them so many lights, benefits, and graces, to bring them to eternal life; for the same end he has redeemed them at the price of so many sorrows and sufferings; and yet they strive to deny all, that they may give free rein to their vicious inclinations! But no: let them strive as they will, the unhappy beings cannot wrest themselves from remorse of conscience, and the dread of the divine vengeance. On this subject I have latterly published a work, entitled The Truth of Faith, in which I have clearly shown the inconsistency of all these systems of modern unbelievers. Oh, if they would but once- forsake sin, and apply themselves earnestly to the love of Jesus Christ, they would then most certainly cast away all doubts about things of faith, and firmly believe all the truths that God has re-vealed!

The true lover of Jesus Christ keeps the eternal truths constantly in view, and orders all his actions according to them. Oh, how thoroughly does he who loves Jesus Christ understand the force of that saying of the Wise Man, *Vanity of vanities, and all is vanity.*1 that all earthly greatness is mere smoke, dirt, and delusion; that the soul's only welfare and happiness consists in loving its

Creator, and in doing his blessed will; that we are, in reality, no more than what we are before God; that it is of no use to gain the whole world, if the soul be lost; that all the goods in the world can never satisfy the human heart, but only God himself; and, therefore, that we must leave all in order to gain all.

1 "Vanitas vanitatum, et omnia vanitas." Eccles. 1.2.

[433] *Charity believes all things.*1 There are other Christians, though not so perverse as the class we have mentioned, who would preferably believe in nothing, that they may give full scope to their unruly passions, and live on undisturbed by the stings of remorse, there are others, I say, who believe, indeed, but their faith is languid; they believe the most holy mysteries of religion, the truths of Revelation contained in the Gospel, the Trinity, the Redemption, the holy Sacraments, and the rest; still they do not believe all. Jesus Christ has said: *Blessed are the poor; blessed are the sorrowful; blessed are the mortified; blessed are those whom men persecute, calumniate and curse. Blessed are the poor; blessed are they that hunger; blessed are they that suffer persecution; blessed are you when men shall revile you, and shall say all manner of evil against you.*2 This is the teaching of Jesus Christ in the Gospel. How, then, can it be said, that those believe in the Gospel who say: "Blessed are those who have money; blessed are those who suffer nothing; blessed are those who can take their amusements; pitiable is the man that suffers persecution and ill-treatment from others"? We must certainly say of such as these, that either they do not believe the Gospel, or that they believe only a part of it. He who believes it all esteems it his highest fortune, and a mark of the divine favor in this world, to be poor, to be sick, to be mortified, to be despised and ill-treated

by men. Such is the belief, and such the language, of one who believes all that is said in the Gospel, and has a real love for Jesus Christ.

Affections and Prayers

My beloved Redeemer, O life of my soul, I firmly believe that You are the only good worthy of being loved. I believe that

1 "Charitas omnia credit."
2 "Beati pauperes. Beati qui lugent. Beati qui esuriunt. Beati qui persecutionem patiuntur. Beati estis cum maledixerint vobis, . . . et dixerint omne malum ad versus vos." Matt. 5.3-11.

[434] You are the greatest lover of my soul, since through love alone You died, overwhelmed with sorrows for love of me. I believe there is no greater blessing in this world, or in the next, than to love You, and to do Your adorable will. All this I be - lieve most firmly; so that I renounce all things, that I may belong wholly to You, and that I may possess You alone. Help me, through the merits of Your sacred Passion, and make me such as You would have me to be. I believe in You, O infallible truth! I trust in You, O infinite mercy! I love You, O infinite goodness! O infinite love, I give myself wholly to You, who have wholly given Yourself to me in Your Passion, and in the holy Sacrament of the Altar.

And I recommend myself to You, O Mary, refuge of sinners, and Mother of God!

CHAPTER XII

LOVE HOPES ALL THINGS
(Hope)
(*Charitas omnia sperat*)

He that loves Jesus Christ hopes for all Things from Him

HOPE increases love, and love increases hope. Hope
in the divine goodness undoubtedly gives an increase
to our love of Jesus Christ. St. Thomas says that in
the very moment when we hope to receive some benefit
from a person, we begin also to love him,1 On this account, the Lord forbids us to put our trust in creatures:
*Put not your trust in princes.*2 Further, he pronounces a
curse on those who do so: *Cursed be the man that trusts
in man.*3 God does not wish us to trust in creatures,

1 "Ex hoc enim quod per aliquem speramus nobis posse provenire
bona, movemur in ipsum sicut in bonum nostrum, et sic incipimus
ipsum amare." *S. Theol.* 1-2, q. 40, a. 7.
2 "Nolite confidere in principibus." Ps. 145.2.
3 "Maledictus homo qui confidit in homine." Jer. 17.5.

[435] because he does not wish us to fix our love upon
them. Hence St. Vincent de Paul said: "Let us beware of
reposing too much confidence in men; for when God beholds us thus leaning on them for support, he himself
withdraws from us." On the other hand, the more we
trust in God, the more we shall advance in his holy love:
*I have run the way of Your commandments, when You
did enlarge my heart.*1 Oh, how rapidly does that soul
advance in perfection that has her heart dilated with
confidence in God! She flies rather than runs; for by

making God the foundation of all her hope, she flings aside her own weakness, and borrows the strength of God himself, which is communicated to all who place their confidence in him: *They that hope in the Lord shall renew their strength, they shall take wings as eagles, they shall run and not be weary, they shall walk and not faint.*2 The eagle is the bird that soars nearest the sun; in like manner, the soul that has God for her trust becomes detached from the earth, and more and more united to God by love.

Now as hope increases the love of God, so does love help to increase hope; for love makes us the adopted sons of God. In the natural order we are the work of his hands; but in the supernatural order we are made sons of God, and partakers of the divine nature, through the merits of Jesus Christ; as the Apostle St. Peter writes: *That by these you may be made partakers of the Divine nature.*3 And if love, makes us the sons of God, it consequently makes us heirs of heaven, according to

1 "Viam mandatorum tuorum cucurri, cum dilatasti cor meum." Ps. 118.32.
2 "Qui autem sperant in Domino, mutabunt fortitudinem, assument pennas sicut aquilae, current et non laborabunt, ambulabunt et non deficient." Is. 40.31.
3 "Ut per haec efficiamini divinae naturae consortes." 2 Pet. 1.4.

[436] St. Paul: *And if sons, heirs also.*1 Now a son claims the right of abiding under the paternal roof; an heir is entitled to the property; and thus love increases the hope of Paradise: so that the souls that love God cry out incessantly, "*Thy kingdom come, Thy kingdom come!*"2 Moreover, God loves those who love him: *I love them that love Me.*3 He showers down his graces on those that seek him by love: *The Lord is good to the soul that seeks*

*Him.*4 Consequently, the soul that loves God most has
the greatest hope in his goodness. This confidence produces that imperturbable tranquility in the saints which
makes them always joyful and full of peace, even amid
the severest trials; for their love of Jesus Christ, and
their persuasion of his liberality towards those who love
him, leads them to trust solely in him; and thus they
find a lasting repose. The sacred spouse abounded with
delights, because she loved none but her Spouse, and
leaned entirely on him for support; she was full of con-
tentment, since she well knew how generous her beloved
is towards all that love him; so that of her it is written:
*Who is this that comes up from the desert, flowing with de-
lights, leaning upon her Beloved?*5 These words of the
Wise Man are most true: *All good things come to me
together with her.*6 With love, all blessings are introduced
into the soul.

The primary object of Christian hope is God, whom
the soul enjoys in the kingdom of heaven. But we must
not suppose that the hope of enjoying God in Paradise
is any obstacle to love; since the hope of Paradise is

1 "Si autem filii, et haeredes." Rom. 8.17.
2 "Adveniat, adveniat regnum tuum."
3 "Ego diligentes me diligo." Prov. 8.17.
4 "Bonus est Dominus. . . . animae quaerenti illum." Lam.3.25.
5 "Quae est ista quae ascendet de deserto, deliciis affluens, innixa
super Dilectum suum?" Song of Songs, 8.5.
6 "Venerunt autem mihi omnia bona pariter cum illa." Wisd. 7.11.

[437] inseparably connected with love, which there receives
its full and complete perfection. Charity is that infinite
treasure, spoken of by the Wise Man, which makes us
the friends of God: *An infinite treasure to men, which they*

*that use become the friends of God.*1 The angelic Doctor
St. Thomas says that friendship is founded on the mutual communication of goods; for as friendship is nothing
more than a mutual love between friends, it follows that
there must be a reciprocal interchange of the good which
each possesses.2 Hence the saint says: "If there be no
communication, there is no friendship." On this account
Jesus Christ says to his disciples: *I have called you friends,
because all things whatsoever I have heard of My Father
I have made known to you.*3 Since he had made them
his friends, he had communicated all his secrets to them.
St. Francis de Sales says: "If, by a supposition of
what is impossible, there could be an infinite good (that
is a God) to whom we belonged in no way whatever,
and with whom we could have no union or communication, we should certainly esteem him more than our
selves; so that we might feel great desire of being able
to love him; but we should not actually love him, be
cause love is built upon union; for love is a friendship,
and the foundation of friendship is to have things in
common; and its end is union."4 Thus St. Thomas
teaches us that love does not exclude the desire of the
reward prepared for us in heaven by Almighty God; on
the contrary, it makes us look to it as the chief object of
our love, for such is God, who constitutes the bliss of

1 "Infinitus enim thesaurus est hominibus, quo qui usi sunt,
participes facti sunt amicitiae Dei." Wisd. 7.14.
2 "Amicitia super amorem addit mutuam redamationem cum
quadam communicatione mutua." *S. Theol.* 1-2, q. 65, a. 5.
3 "Vos autem dixi Amicos, quia omnia, quaecumque audivi a Patre
meo, nota feci vobis." John 15.15.
4 *Love of God,* Bk. 10, ch. 10.

[438] paradise; for friendship implies, that friends rejoice
with one another.1

The Spouse in the Canticles refers to this reciprocal interchange of goods, when she says: *My Beloved to me and I to Him.*2 In heaven the soul belongs wholly to God. and God belongs wholly to the soul, according to the measure of her capacity and of her merits. But from the persuasion which the soul has of her own nothingness in comparison with the infinite attractions of Almighty God, and aware consequently that the claims of God on her love are beyond measure greater than her own can be on the love of God, she is therefore more anxious to procure the divine pleasure than her own enjoyment; so that she is more gratified by the pleasure which she affords Almighty God by giving herself entirely to him, than by God's giving himself entirely to her; but at the same time she is delighted when God thus gives himself to her, inasmuch as she is thereby animated to give herself up to God with a greater intensity, of love. She indeed rejoices at the glory which God imparts to her, but for the sole purpose of referring it back to God himself, and of thus doing her utmost to increase the divine glory. At the sight of God in heaven the soul cannot help loving him with all her strength; on the other hand, God cannot hate any one that loves him: but if (supposing what is impossible) God could hate a soul that loves him, and if a beatified soul could exist without loving God, she would much rather endure all the pains of hell, on condition of being allowed to love God as much as he should hate her, than to live without loving God. even though she could

1 "Amicorum est quod quaerant invicem perfrui; sed nihil aliud est merces nostra, quam perfrui Deo videndo ipsum; ergo charitas, non solum non excludit, sed etiam facit habere oculum ad mercedem." *In 3 Sent.* d. 29, q. 1, a. 4.
2 "Dilectus meus mihi, et ego illi." Song of Songs, 2.16.

[439] enjoy all the other delights of Paradise. So it is; for that conviction which the soul has of God's boundless claims upon her love gives her a greater desire to love God than to be loved by him.

*Charity hopes all things.*1 St. Thomas, with the Master of the Sentences, defines Christian hope to be a "sure expectation of eternal happiness."2 It certainty arises from the infallible promise of God to give eternal life to his faithful servants. Now love, by taking away sin, at the same time takes away all obstacles to our obtaining the happiness of the blessed; hence the greater our love, the greater also and firmer is our hope. hope, on the other hand, can in no way interfere with the purity of love, because, according to the observation of St. Dionysius the Areopagite, love tends naturally to union with the object beloved; or, as St. Augustine asserts in stronger terms, love itself is like a chain of gold that links together the hearts of the lover and the loved. "Love is as it were a kind of bond uniting two together."3 And as this union can never be effected at a distance, the person that loves always longs for the presence of the object of his love. The sacred spouse languished in the absence of her beloved, and entreated her companions to acquaint him with her sorrow, that he might come and console her with his presence: *"I adjure you, O daughters of Jerusalem, if you find my Beloved, that you tell Him that I languish with love."*4 A soul that loves Jesus Christ exceedingly cannot but desire and hope, as long as she remains on earth, to go without delay and be united to her beloved Lord in heaven.

1 "Charitas omnia sperat."
2 "Spes est certa exspectatio beatitudinis." *In 3 Sent.* d. 26.
3 "Amor est quaedam vitta duo aliqua copulans." *De Trin.* Bk. 8,

ch. 10.
4 "Adjuro vos, filiae Jerusalem, si inveneritis Dilectum meum, ut nuntietis ei quia amore langueo." Song of Songs, 5.8.

[440] Thus we see that the desire to go and see God in heaven, not so much for the delight which we shall experience in loving God, as for the pleasure which we shall afford God by loving him, is pure and perfect love. Nor is the joy of the blessed in heaven any hindrance to the purity of their love; such joy is inseparable from their love; but they take far more satisfaction in their love of God than in the joy that it affords them. Some one will perhaps say: But the desire of a reward is rather a love of concupiscence than a love of friendship. We must therefore make a distinction between temporal rewards promised by men and the eternal rewards of paradise promised by God to those who love him: the rewards given by man are distinct from their own persons and independent of them, since they do not bestow themselves, but only their goods, when they would remunerate others; on the contrary, the principal reward which God gives to the blessed is the gift of himself: *I am your reward exceeding great.*1 Hence to desire heaven is the same thing as to desire God, who is our last end.

I wish here to propose a doubt, which may rise in the mind of one who loves God, and strives to conform himself in all things to his blessed will. If it should be ever revealed to such a one that he would be eternally lost, would he be obliged to bow to it with resignation, in order to practice conformity with the will of God? St. Thomas says no; and further, that he would sin by consenting to it, because he would be consenting to live in a state that involves sin, and is contrary to the last end for which God created him; for God did not create

souls to hate him in hell, but to love him in heaven: so
that he does not wish the death even of the sinner, but
that all should be converted and saved. The holy Doctor says that God wishes no one to be damned except

1 "Ego . . . merces tua magna nimis." Gen. 15.1.

[441] through sin; and therefore, a person, by consenting
to his damnation, would not be acting in conformity with
the will of God, but with the will of sin.1 But suppose
that God, foreseeing the sin of a person, should have
decreed his damnation, and that this decree should be
revealed to him, would he be bound to consent to it?
In the same passage the saint says, By no means; be
cause such a revelation must not be taken as an irrevocable decree,- but made merely by way of communication,
as a threat of what would follow if he persists in sin.

But let every one banish such baneful thoughts from
his mind, as only calculated to cool his confidence and
love. Let us love Jesus Christ as much as possible here
below; let us always be sighing to go hence and to behold him in paradise, that we may there love him perfectly; let us make it the grand object of all our hopes,
to go there to love him with all our strength. We are
commanded even in this life to love God with our whole
strength: *You shall love the Lord your God with your whole
heart, with your whole soul, and with all your strength*;2
but the angelical Doctor 3 says that man cannot perfectly
fulfill this precept upon earth; only Jesus Christ, who
was both God and man, and the most holy Mary, who
was full of grace and free from original sin, perfectly
fulfilled it. But we miserable children of Adam, infected
as we are with sin, can not love God without some imperfection; and it is in heaven alone, when we shall see

God face to face, that we shall love him, even more, that we shall be necessitated to love him with all our strength.

Behold, then, the scope of all our desires and aspirations, of all our thoughts and ardent hopes; to go and

1 "Unde, velle suam damnationem absolute, non esset conformare suam voluntatem divinae, sed voluntati peccati." *De Ver.* q. 23, a. 8.
2 "Diliges Dominum Deum tuum ex toto corde tuo, et ex tola anima tua, et ex omnibus viribus tuis," Luke 10.27.
3 *In 3 Sent.* d. 27.

[442] enjoy God in heaven, in order to love him with all our strength, and to rejoice in the enjoyment of God. The blessed certainly rejoice in their own felicity in that kingdom of delights; but the chief source of their happiness, and that which absorbs all the rest, is to know that their beloved Lord possesses an infinite happiness; for they love God incomparably more than themselves. Each one of the blessed has such a love for him, that he would willingly forfeit all happiness, and undergo the most cruel torments, rather than that God should lose (if it were possible for him to lose) one, even the least particle of his happiness. Hence the sight of God's infinite happiness, and the knowledge that it can never suffer diminution for all eternity, constitutes his paradise. This is the meaning of what our Lord says to every soul on whom he bestows the possession of eternal glory: *Enter into the joy of your Lord.*1 It is not the joy that enters into the blessed soul, but the soul that enters into the joy of God, since the joy of God is the object of the joy of the blessed. Thus the good of God will be the good of the blessed; the riches of God will be their riches, and the happiness of God will be their happiness.

On the instant that a soul enters heaven, and sees by
the light of glory the infinite beauty of God face to face,
she is at once seized and all consumed with love. The
happy soul is then as it were lost and immersed in that
boundless ocean of the goodness of God. Then it is
that she quite forgets herself, and inebriated with divine
love, thinks only of loving her God: *They shall be inebriated with the plenty of Your House.*2 As an intoxicated
person no longer thinks of himself, so a soul in bliss can
only think of loving and affording delight to her beloved
Lord; she desires to possess him entirely, and she does

1 "Intra in gaudium Domini tui." Matt. 25.21.
2 "Inebriabuntur ab ubertate domus tuae." Ps. 35.9.

[443] in fact possess him, without fear of losing him any
more; she desires to give herself wholly to him, at every
moment, and she does indeed possess him for every moment she offers herself to God without reserve, and God
receives her in his loving embraces, and so holds her, and
shall hold her in the same fond embraces for all eternity.

In this manner the soul is wholly united to God in
heaven, and loves him with all her strength; her love is
most perfect and complete, and though necessarily finite,
since a creature is not capable of infinite love, it nevertheless renders her perfectly happy and contented, so
that she desires nothing more. On the other hand, Almighty God communicates himself, and unites himself
wholly to the soul, filling her with himself proportion-
ately to her merits; and this union is not merely by
means only of his gifts, lights, and loving attractions, as
is the case during the present life, but by his own very
essence. As fire penetrates iron, and seems to change it
into itself, so does God penetrate the soul and fill her

with himself; and though she never loses her own being,
yet she becomes so penetrated and absorbed by that
immense ocean of the divine substance, that she remains,
as it were, annihilated, and as if she ceased to exist.
The Apostle prayed for this happy lot for his disciples
when he said: *That you may be filled unto all the fullness
of God.*1

And this is the last end, which the goodness of God
has appointed for us in the life to come. Hence the soul
can never enjoy perfect repose on earth; because it is
only in heaven that she can obtain perfect union with
God. It is true that the lovers of Jesus Christ find peace
in the practice of perfect conformity with the will of
God; but they cannot in this life find complete repose;

1 "Ut impleamini in omnem plenitudinem Dei." Eph. 2.19.

[444] this is only obtained when our last end is obtained;
that is, when we see God face to face, and are consumed
with his divine love; and as long as the soul does not reach
this end, she is ill at ease, and groans and sighs, saying:
*Behold, in peace is my bitterness most bitter.*1 Yes, O my
God, I live in peace in this valley of tears, because such
is Your will; but I cannot help feeling unspeakable bitterness at finding myself at a distance from You, and
not yet perfectly united with You, who are my center,
my all, and the fullness of my repose!

For this reason the saints, though they were all in
flamed with the love of God, did nothing but sigh after
paradise. David cried out: *Woe is me, that my sojourning is prolonged!*2 *I shall be satisfied when your glory
shall appear.*3 St. Paul said of himself: *Having a desire
to be with Christ.*4 St. Francis of Assisi said:

"Such are the joys that lure my sight,
All pains grow sweet, all labors light."5

These were all so many acts of perfect love. The
angelic Doctor teaches us, that the highest degree of
love that a soul can reach upon earth, is to desire in-
tensely to go and be united with God, and to enjoy him
in heaven.6 But, as we have already seen, this enjoyment of God in heaven does not consist so much in the
fruition of the delights there lavished on her by Almighty God, as in the pleasure she takes in the happiness of God himself, whom she loves incomparably more
than herself.

1 "Ecce in pace amaritudo mea amarissima." Is. 38.17.
2 "Heu mihi, quia incolatus meus prolongatus est." Ps. 119.5.
3 "Satiabor cum apparuerit gloria tua." Ps. 16.15.
4 "Desiderium habens dissolvi, et esse cum Christo." Phil. 1.23.
5 "Tanto `e il bene ch' io aspetto Ch' ogni pena m'e diletto."
Apophth. 57.
6 "Tertium autem studium est ut homo ad hoc principaliter intendat,
ut Deo inhaereat et eo fruatur; et hoc pertinet ad perfectos, qui cupi-
unt dissolvi, et esse cum Christo." *S. Theol.* 2-2, q. 24, a. 9.

[445] The holy souls in purgatory feel no pain more acutely
than that of their yearning to possess God, from whom
they remain still at a distance. And this sort of pain
will afflict those especially who in their lifetime had but
little desire of paradise. Cardinal Bellarmine 1 also says,
that there is a certain place in purgatory called, prison
of honor,2 where certain souls are not tormented with
any pain of sense, but merely with the pain of privation
of the sight of God; examples of this are related by St.
Gregory, Venerable Bede, St. Vincent Ferrer, and St.
Bridget; and this punishment is not for the commission

of sin, but for coldness in desiring heaven. Many souls aspire to perfection; but for the rest, they are too indifferent whether they go to enjoy the sight of God, or continue on earth. But eternal life is an inestimable good, that has been purchased by the death of Jesus Christ; and God punishes such souls as have been remiss during life in their desires to obtain it.

Affections and Prayers

O God, my Creator and my Redeemer, You have created me for heaven; You have redeemed me from hell to bring me into heaven; and I have so many times, in Your very face, renounced my claim to heaven by my sins, and have remained contented in seeing myself doomed to hell! But blessed forever be Your infinite mercy, which, I would eagerly hope, has pardoned me, and many a time rescued me from perdition. Ah, my Jesus, would that I had never offended You! would that I had always loved You! I am glad that at least I have still time to do so. I love You! O love of my soul, I love You with my whole heart; I love You more than myself! I see plainly that You wish to save me, that I may be able to love You for all eternity in that kingdom of love. I thank You, and beseech You to help me for the remainder of my life, in which I wish to love You most ardently, that I may ardently love You in eternity. Ah, my Jesus, when will the day arrive that shall free me from all

1 *On Purgatory*, Bk. 2, ch. 7.
2 "Carcer honoratus."

[446] danger of losing You, that, shall consume me with love, by unveiling before my eyes Your infinite beauty, so that I shall be under the necessity of loving You? Oh, sweet necessity! oh, happy and dear and most desired necessity, which shall relieve me from all fear of evermore displeasing You, and shall oblige me to love You with all my strength! My conscience alarms

me, and says: "How can You presume to enter heaven?"
But, my dearest Redeemer, Your merits are all my hope.

O Mary, Queen of Heaven, your intercession is all-powerful
with God , in you I put my trust!

CHAPTER 13

LOVE ENDURES ALL THINGS
(Perseverance)
(Charitas omnia sustinet)

**He that loves Jesus Christ with a Strong Love
does not cease to love Him in the midst of all
Sorts of Temptations and Desolations.**

IT is not the pains of poverty, of sickness, of dishonor
and persecution, which in this life most afflict the souls
that love God, but temptations and desolations of spirit.
While a soul is in the enjoyment of the loving presence of God, she is so far from grieving at all the afflictions and disgraces and outrages of men, that she is
rather comforted by them, as they afford her an opportunity of showing God a token of her love; they serve,
in short, as fuel to enkindle her love more and more.
But to find herself solicited by temptations to forfeit the
divine grace, or in the hour of desolation to apprehend
having already lost it, oh, these are torments too cruel
to bear for one who loves Jesus Christ with all her heart!
However, the same love supplies her with strength to
endure all patiently, and to pursue the way of perfection,
on which she has entered. And, oh, what progress do
[447] those souls make by means of these trials, which
God is pleased to send them in order to prove their love!

1. Temptations

Temptations are the most grievous trials that can
happen to a soul that loves Jesus Christ; she accepts
with resignation of every other evil, as calculated only
to bind her in closer union with God; but temptations

to commit sin would drive her, as we said above, to a separation from Jesus Christ; and on this account they are more intolerable to her than all other afflictions.

Why God permits Temptations

We must know, however, that although no temptation to evil can ever come from God, but only from the devil or our own corrupt inclinations: *for God is not a tempter of evils, and he tempts no man*;1 nevertheless, God does at times permit his most cherished souls to be the most grievously tempted.

In the first place, in order that from temptations the soul may better learn her own weakness, and the need she has of the divine assistance not to fall. While a soul is favored with heavenly consolations, she feels as if she were able to vanquish every assault of the enemy, and to achieve every undertaking for the glory of God. But when she is strongly tempted, and is almost reeling on the edge of the precipice, and just ready to fall, then she becomes better acquainted with her own misery and with her inability to resist, if God did not come to her rescue. So it fared with St. Paul, who tells us that God had suffered him to be troubled with a temptation to sensual pleasure, in order to keep him humble after the revelations with which God had favored him: *And lest the*

1 "Deus enim intentator malorum est, ipse autem neminem tentat." James 1.13.

[448] *greatness of the revelations should exalt me, there was given me a sting of my flesh, an angel of Satan to buffet me.*1

Besides, God permits temptations with a view to detach us more thoroughly from this life; and to kindle in us the desire to go and behold him in heaven. Hence pious souls, finding themselves attacked day and night by so many enemies, come at length to feel a loathing for life, and exclaim: *Woe is me, that my sojourning is prolonged!*2 And they sigh for the moment when they can say: *The snare is broken and we are delivered.*3 The soul would willingly wing her flight to God; but as long as she lives upon this earth she is bound by a snare which detains her here below, where she is continually assailed with temptations; this snare is only broken by death: so that the souls that love God sigh for death, which will deliver them from all danger of losing him.

Almighty God, moreover, allows us to be tempted, to make us richer in merits; as it was said to Tobias: *And because you were acceptable to God, it was necessary that temptations should prove you.*4 Thus a soul need not imagine herself out of God's favor because she is tempted, but should make it rather a motive of hope that God loves her. It is a delusion of the devil to lead some pusillanimous persons to suppose that temptations are sins that contaminate the soul. It is not bad thoughts that make us lose God, but the consenting to them; let the suggestions of the devil be ever so violent, let those filthy imaginations which overload our minds be ever so lively, they cannot cast the least stain on our souls, provided only we yield no consent to them; on the contrary, they

1 "Et ne magnitude revelationum extollat me, datus est mihi stimulus carnis meae, angelus Satanae, qui me colaphizet." 2 Cor. 12.7.
2 "Heu mihi, quia incolatus meus prolongatus est." Ps. 119.5.

3 "Laqueus contritus est, et nos liberati sumus." Ps. 123.7.
4 "Et quia acceptus eras Deo, necesse fuit, ut tentatio probaret te."
Tob. 12.13.

[449] make the soul purer, stronger, and dearer to Almighty God. St. Bernard says that every time we overcome a temptation we win a fresh crown in heaven:
"As often as we conquer, so often are we crowned."1
An angel once appeared to a Cistercian monk, and put
a crown into his hands, with orders that he should carry
it to one of his fellow-religious, as a reward for the
temptation that he had lately overcome.

Nor must we be disturbed if evil thoughts do not immediately disappear from our minds, but continue obstinately to persecute us; it is enough if we detest them,
and do our best to banish them. God is faithful, says
the Apostle; he will not allow us to be tempted above
our strength: *God is faithful, who will not allow you to be
tempted above that which you are able; but will make also
with temptation provision, that you may be able to bear it.*2
Thus a person, so far from losing anything by temptations,
derives great profit from them. On this account God frequently allows the souls dearest to him to undergo the
severest temptations, that they may turn them into a source
of greater merit on earth, and of greater glory in heaven.
Stagnant water soon grows putrid; a soul left at ease,
without any struggle or temptation, stands in great
danger of perishing from some self-conceit of her own
merit; she perhaps imagines herself to have already attained to perfection, and therefore has little fear; and
consequently takes little pains to recommend herself to
God and to secure her salvation; but when, on the contrary, she is agitated by temptations, and sees herself in
danger of rushing headlong into sin, then she has recourse

to God; she goes to the divine Mother; she renews her
resolution rather to die than to sin; she humbles herself,

1 "Quoties restiteris, toties coronaberis." *On Lent*, sermon 5.
2 "Fidelis autem Deus est, qui non patietur vos tentari supra id quod
 potestis, sed faciet etiam cum tentatione proventum." 1 Cor. 10.13.

[450] and casts herself into the arms of the divine mercy:
in this manner, as experience shows us, the soul acquires
fresh strength and closer union with God.

This must not, however, lead us to seek after temptations; on the contrary, we must pray to God to deliver
us from temptations, and from those more especially by
which God foresees we should be overcome; and this is
precisely the object of that petition of the Our Father:
Lead us not into temptation;[1] but when, by God's permission, we are beset with temptations, we must then, without either being alarmed or discouraged by those foul
thoughts, rely wholly on Jesus Christ, and beseech him
to help us; and he, on his part, will not fail to give us
the strength to resist. St. Augustine says: "Throw
yourself on him, and fear not; he will not withdraw to
let you fall."[2]

Remedies against Temptations

Let us come now to the means which we have to employ in order to vanquish temptations. Spiritual masters prescribe a variety of means; but the most necessary,
and the safest (of which only I will here speak), is to
have immediate recourse to God with all humility and
confidence, saying: *Incline unto my aid, O God; O Lord,
make haste to help me!*[3] This short prayer will enable us

to overcome the assaults of all the devils of hell; for God is infinitely more powerful than all of them. Almighty God knows well that of ourselves we are unable to resist the temptations of the infernal powers; and on this account the most learned Cardinal Gotti remarks, "that whenever we are assailed, and in danger of being

1 "Et ne nos inducas in tentationem." Matt. 6.13.
2 "Projice te in eum, noli metuere; non se subtrahet, ut cadas." *Confessions*, Bk. 8, ch. 11.
3 "Deus, in adjutorium meum intende; Domine, ad adjuvandum me festina." Ps. 69.2.

[451] overcome, God is obliged to give us strength enough to resist as often as we call upon him for it."1

And how can we doubt of receiving help from Jesus Christ, after all the promises that he has made us in the Holy Scriptures? *Come to Me, all you that labor and are heavy laden, and I will refresh you.*2 Come to me, you who are wearied in fighting against temptations, and I will restore your strength. *Call upon Me in the day of trouble: I will deliver you, and you shall honor Me.*3 When you see yourself troubled by your enemies, call upon me, and I will bring you out of the danger, and you shall praise me. *Then shall you call, and the Lord shall hear: you shall cry, and He shall say, Here I am.*4 Then shall you call upon the Lord for help, and he will hear you: you shall cry out, Quick, O Lord, help me! and he will say to you, Behold, here I am; I am present to help you. *Who has called upon Him, and He despised him?*5 And who, says the prophet, has ever called upon God, and God has despised him without giving him help? David felt sure of never falling a prey to his enemies, while he could have recourse to prayer; he says: *Praising, I will*

*call upon the Lord: and I shall be saved from my enemies.*6
For he well knew that God is close to all who invoke his
aid: *The Lord is near unto all them that call upon Him.*7

1 "Respondeo, . . . cum tentamur, nobis ad Deum confugientibus, per
gratiam a Deo paratam et oblatam, vires adfuturas, qua possimus
resistere et actu resistamus." *De Divinae Gratia,* q. 2, d. 5, par. 3.
2 "Venite ad me omnes, qui, laboratis et onerati estis, et ego reficiam
vos." Matt. 11.28.
3 "Et invoca me in die tribulationis; eruam te, et honorificabis me."
Ps. 49.15.
4 "Tune invocabis, et Dominus exaudiet; clamabis, et dicet: Ecce
adsum." Is. 58.9.
5 "Quis invocavit eum, et despexit illum? Ecclus. (Sirach) 2.12.
6 "Laudans invocabo Dominum, et ab inimicis meis salvus ero."
Ps. 17.4.
7 "Prope est Dominus omnibus invocantibus eum." Ps. 144.18.

[452] And St. Paul adds, that the Lord is by no means
sparing, but lavish of graces towards all that pray to him:
*Rich unto all that call upon Him.*1

Oh, would to God that all men would have recourse
to him whenever they are tempted to offend him; they
would then certainly never commit sin! They unhappily
fall, because, led away by the cravings of their vicious
appetites, they prefer to lose God, the sovereign good,
than to forego their wretched short-lived pleasures. Experience gives us manifest proofs that whoever calls on
God in temptation does not fall; and whoever fails to
call on him as surely falls: and this is especially true of
temptations to impurity. Solomon himself said that he
knew very well he could not be chaste, unless God gave
him the grace to be so; and he therefore invoked him by
prayer in the moment of temptation: *And as I knew that I
could not otherwise be continent, except God gave it, . . .*

*I went to the Lord and besought Him.*2 In temptations against purity (and the same holds good with regard to those
against faith), we must take it as a rule never to strive
to combat the temptation hand to hand; but we must
endeavor immediately to get rid of it indirectly by making a good act of the love of God or of sorrow for our
sins, or else by applying ourselves to some indifferent
occupation calculated to distract us. At the very instant
that we discover a thought of evil tendency, we must
disown it immediately, and (so to speak) close the door
in its face, and deny it all entrance into the mind, with
out tarrying in the least to examine its object or errand.
We must cast away these foul suggestions as quickly as
we would shake off a hot spark from the fire.

If the impure temptation has already forced its way

1 "Dives in omnibus qui invocant illum." Rom. 10.12.
2 "Et ut scivi quoniam aliter non possem esse continens, nisi
Deus det, . . . adii Dominum, et deprecatus sum illum." Wisd. 8.21.

[453] into the mind, and plainly pictures its object to the
imagination, so as to stir the passions, then, according to
the advice of St. Jerome, we must burst forth into these
words: "O Lord, You are my helper."1 As soon, says
the saint, as we feel the sting of concupiscence, we must
have recourse to God, and say: "O Lord, do You assist
me;" we must invoke the most holy names of Jesus and
Mary, which possess a wonderful efficacy in the suppres-
sion of temptations of this nature. St. Francis de Sales
says that no sooner do children espy a wolf than they
instantly seek refuge in the arms of their father and
mother; and there they remain out of all danger. Our
conduct must be the same: we must flee without delay
for help to Jesus and Mary, by earnestly calling upon

them. I repeat that we must instantly have recourse to
them, without giving a moment's audience to the temptation, or disputing with it. It is related in the fourth
paragraph of the Book of Sentences of the Fathers,2 that
one day St. Pacomius heard the devil boasting that he had
frequently got the better of a certain monk on account
of his lending ear to him, and not turning instantly to
call upon God. He heard another devil, on the contrary,
utter this complaint: As for me, I can do nothing with
my monk, because he never fails to have recourse to God,
and always defeats me.

Should the temptation, however, obstinately persist in
attacking us, let us beware of becoming troubled or
angry at it; for this might put it in the power of our
enemy to overcome us. We must, on such occasions,
make an act of humble resignation to the will of God,
who thinks fit to allow us to be tormented by these
abominable temptations; and we must say: O Lord, I
deserve to be molested with these filthy suggestions, in

1 "Statim ut libido titillaverit sensum, erumpamus in vocem:
Dominus auxiliator meus!" *Letter to Eustochium.*
2 *Lives of the Fathers*, Bk. 3, n. 35.

[454] punishment of my past sins; but You must help to
free me. And as long as the temptation lasts, let us never
cease calling on Jesus and Mary. It is also very profit
able, in the like importunity of temptations, to renew our
firm resolve to God of suffering every torment, and a
thousand deaths, rather than offend him; and at the same
time we must invoke his divine assistance. And even
should the temptation be of such violence as to put us in
imminent risk of consenting to it, we must then redouble
our prayers, hasten into the presence of the Blessed

Sacrament, cast ourselves at the feet of the crucifix, or of some image of our Blessed Lady, and there pray with in creased fervor, and cry out for help with groans and tears. God is certainly ready to hear all who pray to him; and it is from him alone, and not from our own exertions, that we must look for strength to resist; but sometimes Almighty God wills these struggles of us, and then he makes up for our weakness, and grants us the victory. It is an excellent practice also, in the moment of temptation, to make the sign of the cross on the forehead and breast. It is also of great service to discover the temptation to our spiritual director. St. Philip Neri used to say, that a temptation disclosed is half overcome.

Here it will be well to remark, what is unanimously admitted by all theologians, even of the rigorist school, that persons who have during a considerable period of time been leading a virtuous life, and live habitually in the fear of God, whenever they are in doubt, and are not certain whether they have given consent to a grievous sin, ought to be perfectly assured that they have not lost the divine grace; for it is morally impossible that the will, confirmed in its good purposes for a consider able lapse of time, should on a sudden undergo so total a change as at once to consent to a mortal sin without clearly knowing it; the reason of it is, that mortal sin is so horrible a monster that it cannot possible enter a soul [455] by which it has long been held in abhorrence, without her being fully aware of it. We have proved this at length in our Moral Theology.1 St. Teresa said: No one is lost without knowing it; and no one is deceived with out the will to be deceived.2

Wherefore, with regard to certain souls of delicate con- science, and solidly rooted in virtue, but at the same time timid and molested with temptations (especially if they be against faith or chastity), the director will find it sometimes expedient to forbid them to discover them or make any mention of them; because, if they have to mention them they are led to consider how such thoughts got entrance into their minds, and whether they paused to dispute with them, or took any complacency in them, or gave any consent to them; and so, by this too great reflection, those evil imaginations make a still deeper impression on their minds, and disturb them the more, Whenever the confessor is morally certain that the penitent has not consented to these suggestions, the best way is to forbid him to speak any more about them. And I find that St. Jane Frances de Chantal acted precisely in this manner. She relates of herself, that she was for several years assailed by the most violent storms of temptation, but had never spoken of them in confession, since she was not conscious of having ever yielded to them; and in this she had only followed faithfully the rule received from her director. She says, "I never had a full conviction of having consented."3 These words give us to understand that the temptations did produce in her some agitation from scruples; but in spite of these, she resumed her tranquility on the strength of the obedience imposed by her confessor, not to confess similar doubts. With this exception, it will be generally found an ad-

1 Bk. 6, n. 476.
2 *Life*, additions.
3 *Mem. de la M. de Chaugy*, Pt. 3, ch. 27.

[456] mirable means of quelling the violence of temptations to lay them open to our director, as we have said above.

But I repeat, the most efficacious and the most necessary of all remedies against temptations, is that remedy of all remedies, namely, to pray to God for help, and to continue praying as long as the temptation continues. Almighty God will frequently have decreed success, not to the first prayer, but to the second, third, or fourth. In short, we must be thoroughly persuaded that all our welfare depends on prayer: our amendment of life depends on prayer; our victory over temptations depends on prayer; on prayer depends our obtaining divine love, together with perfection, perseverance, and eternal salvation.

There may be some who, after the perusal of my spiritual works, will accuse me of tediousness in so often recommending the importance and necessity of having continual recourse to God by prayer. But I seem to myself to have said not too much, but far too little. I know that day and night we are all assailed with temptations from the infernal powers, and that Satan lets slip no occasion of causing us to fall. I know that, without the divine help, we have not strength to repel the assaults of the devils; and that therefore the Apostle exhorts us to put on the armor of God: Put you on the armor of God, that you may be able to stand against the deceits of the devil. For our wrestling is not against flesh and blood; but against principalities and powers, against the rulers of the world of this darkness? And what is this armor with which St. Paul warns us to clothe ourselves in order to conquer our enemies? Behold of what it consists: *By all prayer and supplication, praying at all times in the spirit, and in the same*

1 "Induite vos armaturam Dei, ut possitis stare adversus insidias diaboli; quoniam non est nobis colluctatio adversus carnem et sanguinem, sed adversus principes et potestates, adversus mundi rectores tenebrarum harum." Eph. 6.11, 12.

[457] *watching with all instance.*1 This armor is constant and fervent prayer to God, that he may help us to gain the victory. I know, moreover, that in every page of the Holy Scriptures, both in the Old and the New Testament, we are repeatedly admonished to pray: *Call upon Me, and I will deliver you.*2 *Cry to Me, and I will hear you.*3 *We ought always to pray, and not to faint.*4 *Ask, and you shall receive.*5 *Watch and pray.*6 *Pray without ceasing.*7 So that I think, far from having spoken too much on prayer, I have not said enough.

I would urge it on all preachers, to recommend nothing so much to their audience as prayer; on confessors, to insist on nothing so earnestly with their penitents as prayer; on spiritual writers, to treat on no subject more copiously than on prayer. But it is a source of grief to my heart, and it seems to me a chastisement of our sins, that so many preachers, confessors, and authors speak so little of prayer. There is no doubt that sermons, meditations, Communions, and mortifications are great helps in the spiritual life; but if we fail to call upon God by prayer in the moment of temptation, we shall fall, in spite of all the sermons, meditations, Communions, penances, and virtuous resolutions. If, then, we really wish to be saved, let us always pray, and commend ourselves to Jesus Christ, and most of all when we are tempted; and let us not only pray for the grace of holy perseverance, but at the same time for the grace to pray always. Let us, likewise, take care to recommend ourselves to the divine Mother, who, as St. Bernard says, is the dispenser

1 "Per omnem orationem et obsecrationem orantes omni tempore in spiritu, et in ipso vigilantes in omni instantia." Eph. 6.18.
2 "Invoca me . . . eruam te." Ps. 49.15.
3 "Clama ad me, et exaudiam te." Jer. 33.3.

4 "Oportet semper orare et non deficere." Luke 18.1.
5 "Petite, et dabitur vobis." Matt. 7.7.
6 "Vigilate et orate." Matt. 26.41.
7 "Sine intermissione orate." 1 Thess. 5.17.

[458] of graces: "Let us seek for graces, and let us seek them through Mary."1 For the same saint assures us that it is the will of God, that not a single grace should be dealt to us except through the hands of Mary: "God has willed us to receive nothing that has not passed through the hands of Mary."2

Affections and Prayers

O Jesus, My Redeemer, I trust in Your blood, that You have forgiven me all my offenses against You; and I fondly hope to come one day to bless You for it eternally in heaven: *The mercies of the Lord I will sing forever*.3 I plainly see now that I have over and over again fallen in times past, from the not entreating You for holy perseverance. I earnestly beg You at this present moment to grant me perseverance: "Never permit me to be separated from You."4 And I resolve to make this prayer to You always; but especially when I am tempted to offend You. I indeed make this resolution and promise; but what will it profit me thus to resolve and promise, if You do not give me the grace to run and cast myself at Your feet? By the merits, then, of Your sacred Passion, oh, grant me this grace, in all my necessities to have recourse to You.
Mary, my Queen, and my Mother, I beseech you, by your tender love for Jesus Christ, to procure me the grace of always fleeing for help, as long as I live, to your blessed Son and to you.

2. Desolations

St. Francis de Sales says: "It is a mistake to estimate

devotions by the consolations which we feel. True
devotion in the way of God consists in having a determined will to execute all that is pleasing to God."5 Al-

1 "Quaeramus gratiam, et per Mariam quaeramus."
2 "Nihil nos Deus voluit habere, quod per Mariae manus non
transiret." *On the Vigil of Christmas*, sermon 3.
3 "Misericordias Domini in aeternum cantabo." Ps. 88.2.
4 "Ne permittas me separari a te."
5 *Introduction to the Devout Life*, ch. 13.

[459] mighty God will often make use of aridities in order
to draw closer to him his most cherished souls. Attachment to our own disordered inclinations is the greatest
obstacle to true union with God; and when, therefore,
God intends to draw a soul to his perfect love, he endeavors to detach her from all affection to created goods.
Thus his first care is to deprive her of temporal goods,
of worldly pleasures, of property, honors, friends, relatives, and bodily health; by the like means of losses,
troubles, neglects, bereavements, and infirmities, he ex-
tirpates by degrees all earthly attachment, in order that
the affections may beset on him alone.

With a view to produce a fondness for spiritual things,
God regales the soul at first with great consolations, with
an abundance of tears and tenderness; she is thus easily
weaned from the gratifications of sense, and seeks further
to mortify herself with works of penance, fasts, hair-
shirts, and disciplines; at this stage the director must
keep a check on her, and not allow her to practice mortifications at least not all those for which she asks permission because, under the spur of this sensible devotions, a soul might easily ruin her health by indiscretion.
It is a subtle artifice of the devil, when he beholds a per-

son giving himself up to God, and receiving the consolations and caresses which God generally gives to begin
ners, to do his utmost to plunge him into the performance
of immoderate penances, so as utterly to destroy his
health; so that afterwards, by reason of bodily weakness,
he not only gives up the mortifications, but prayer, Communion, and all exercises of devotion, and eventually
sinks back into his old way of living. On this account,
the director should be very sparing in allowing mortifications to those who are only just entering upon the
spiritual life, and who desire to practice bodily mortifications; let him exhort them to practice rather interior
mortification, by bearing patiently with insults and
[460] contradictions, by obedience to Superiors, by bridling
the curiosity to see, to hear, and the like; and let him
tell them, that when they have acquired the good habit
of practicing these interior mortifications, they will then
be sufficiently perfect to proceed to the external ones. For
the rest, it is a serious error to say, as some say, that external mortifications are of little or no use. Without doubt,
interior mortification is most requisite for perfection; but
it does not follow from this that external mortifications
are unnecessary. St. Vincent de Paul declared that the
person who does not practice external mortifications will
be neither mortified interiorly nor exteriorly. And St.
John of the Cross declared that the director who despised
external mortifications was unworthy of confidence, even
though he should work miracles.

But to come back to our point. The soul then, in the
commencement of her conversion to God, tastes the
sweetness of those sensible consolations with which God
seeks to allure her, and by them to wean her from
earthly pleasures; she breaks off her attachment to
creatures, and becomes attached to God. Still, her at-

tachment is imperfect, inasmuch as it is fostered more
by that sensibility of spiritual consolations than by the
real wish to do what is pleasing to God; and she deceives herself by believing that the greater the pleasure
she feels in her devotions, the more she loves Almighty
God. The consequence of this is, that if this food of
spiritual consolations is stopped, by her being taken
from her ordinary exercises of devotion, and employed
in other works of obedience, love, or duties of her
state, she is disturbed, and takes it greatly to heart:
and this is a universal defect in our miserable human
nature, to seek our own satisfaction in all that we do. Or
again, when she no longer finds this sweet relish of devotion in her exercises, she either forsakes them, or lessens
them; and continuing to lessen them from day to day,
[461] she at length omits them entirely. And this misfortune
befalls many souls who, when called by Almighty God to
love him, enter upon the way of perfection, and as long
as spiritual sweetness lasts, make a certain progress;
but alas! when this is no longer tasted, they leave off
all, and resume their former ways. But it is of the highest importance to be fully persuaded that the love of
God and perfection do not consist in feelings of tender
ness and consolation, but in overcoming self-love, and
in following the divine will. St. Francis de Sales says:
"God is as worthy of our love when he afflicts us as
when he consoles us."

Amid these consolations, it requires no remarkable
degree of virtue to forego sensual delights, and to endure insults and contradictions. The soul in the midst
of these sweetnesses can endure all things; but this endurance comes far more frequently from those sensible
consolations than from the strength of true love of God.
On this account the Lord, with a view to give her a solid

foundation in virtue, retires from her, and deprives her of that sensible devotion, that he may rid her of all attachment to self-love, which was fed by such consolations. And hence it happens, that whereas formerly she felt a joy in making acts of offering, of confidence, and of love, now that the vein of consolations is dried up, she makes these acts with coldness and painful effort; and finds a weariness in the most pious exercises, in her prayers, spiritual readings, and Communions; she even finds in them nothing but darkness and fears, and all seems lost to her. She prays and prays again, and is overwhelmed with sadness, because God seems to have abandoned her.

Let us come now to the practice of what we are to do on our part in the like circumstances. When Almighty God in his mercy deigns to console us with his loving visitations, and to let us feel the presence of his grace, [462] it is not good to reject the divine consolations, as some false mystics advise: let us thankfully receive them; but let us beware of settling down on them, and seeking delight in those feelings of spiritual tenderness. St. John of the Cross calls this a "spiritual gluttony," which is faulty and displeasing to God. Let us strive in such moments to banish from our mind the sensible enjoyment of these sweetnesses: and let us be especially on our guard against supposing that these favors are a token of our standing better with God than others; for such a thought of vanity would oblige God to withdraw himself from us altogether, and to leave us in our miserries. We must certainly at such times return most fervent thanks to God, because such spiritual consolations are signal gifts of the divine bounty to our souls, far greater than all the riches and honors of this world; but let us not seek then to regale ourselves on these sen-

sible sweetnesses, but let us rather humble ourselves by
the remembrance of the sins of our past life. For the
rest, we must consider this loving treatment as the pure
result of the goodness of God; and that perhaps it is
sent as the forerunner of some great tribulation soon to
befall us, in order that we may be strengthened by these
consolations to endure all with patience and resignation.
We should therefore take the occasion of offering ourselves to suffer every pain, internal or external, that may
happen to us, every illness, every persecution, every
spiritual desolation, saying: O my Lord, I am here before You; do with me, and with all that belongs to me,
whatever You will; grant me the grace to love You
and perfectly to accomplish Your holy will, and I ask no
more!

When a soul is morally certain of being in the grace
of God, although she may be deprived of worldly pleasures, as well as of those which come from God, she
nevertheless rests satisfied with her state, conscious, as
[463] she is, of loving God, and of being loved by him. But
God, who wishes to see. her purified and divested of all
sensible satisfaction, in order to unite her entirely to
himself by means of pure love, what does he do? He
puts her in the crucible of desolation, which is more
painful to bear than the most severe trials, whether internal or external; she is left in a state of uncertainty if
she be in the grace of God or not, and in the dense darkness that shrouds her, there seems no prospect of her
evermore finding God. Almighty God, moreover, will
sometimes permit her to be assailed by violent sensual
temptations, accompanied by irregular movements of
the inferior part, or perhaps by thoughts of unbelief, of
despair, and even of hatred of God, when she imagines
herself cast off by him, and that he no longer hears her

prayers. And as, on the one hand, the suggestions of
the devil are vehement, and the motions of concupiscence are excited, and, on the other, the soul finds her
self in this great darkness, she can no longer sufficiently
distinguish whether she properly resists or yields to the
temptations, though her will resolutely refuses all consent. Her fears of having lost God are thus very much
increased; and from her fancied infidelity in struggling
against the temptations, she thinks herself deservedly
abandoned by God. The saddest of all calamities seems
to have befallen her, to be able no longer to love God,
and to be hated by him. St. Teresa passed through all
these trials, and declares that during them solitude had
no charms for her, but, on the contrary, filled her with
horror; while prayer was changed for her into a perfect hell.

When a soul that loves God finds herself in this state,
she must not lose courage; and neither must he who directs her become alarmed. Those sensual movements,
those temptations against faith, those feelings of dis-
trust, and those attacks which urge her to hate Almighty
[464] God, are fears, are tortures of the soul, are efforts
of the enemy; but they are not voluntary, and therefore they
are not sins. The sincere lover of Jesus Christ resists
valiantly on such occasions, and withholds all consent
to such suggestions; but because of the darkness which
envelops her, she knows not how to distinguish, her
soul is thrown into confusion, and the privation of the
presence of divine grace makes her fearful and sad. But
it can be soon discovered that in these souls, thus tried
by God, all is dread and apprehension, but not truth:
only ask them, even in their state of desolation, whether
they would willingly commit one single deliberate venial
sin; they will answer, that they are ready to suffer not

one, but a thousand deaths, rather than be guilty of such displeasure to Almighty God.

It is necessary, therefore, to make this distinction, that it is one thing to perform an act of virtue, such as to repel a temptation, to trust in God, to love God, and to will what he wills; and it is another thing to have the consciousness of really making these good acts. This consciousness of doing good contributes to our pleasure; but the profit consists in the first point, that is, in actually doing good. With the first God is satisfied, and deprives the soul of the latter that is, of the consciousness of doing good, in order thus to remove from her all self-satisfaction, which adds nothing to the merit of the action; for our Lord seeks more our real advantage than our own satisfaction. St. John of the Cross wrote the following words of comfort to a desolate soul: "You were never in a better state than at present; for you were never so deeply humbled, and so cut off from all attachment to this world, and at the same time you were never so thoroughly impressed with the conviction of your own wickedness. Neither were you ever so divested and purified of all self-seeking as now."1 Let us,

1 *Letter* 8.

[465] then, not believe that when we feel a greater tenderness of devotion we are more beloved by God; for perfection does not consist in that, but in the mortification of our own will, and in its union with the will of God.

Wherefore, in this state of desolation the soul must not heed the devil, when he suggests that God has abandoned her; nor must she leave off prayer. This is the object at which the devil is aiming, in order afterwards to drag her down some precipice. St. Teresa writes: "The Lord proves his true lovers by dryness and temptations. What though the dryness should be of life long duration, let the soul never relax in prayer; the time will arrive when all will be abundantly repaid."1 In such a state of suffering, a person should humble himself by the reflection that his offenses against God are undeserving of any milder treatment: he should humble himself, and be fully resigned to the divine will, saying: O my Lord, behold me at Your feet; if it be Your will that I should remain thus desolate and afflicted for my whole life, and even for all eternity, only grant me Your grace and the gift of Your love, and do with me whatever You will.

It will be useless then, and perhaps a source of greater disquiet, to wish to assure yourself that you are in the grace of God, and that what you experience is only a trial, and not abandonment on the part of God. At such times it is not the will of God that you should have this assurance; and he so wills it for your greater advantage, in order that you may humble yourself the more, and increase your prayers and acts of confidence in his mercy. You desire to see, and God wills that you should not see. For the rest, St. Francis de Sales says: "The resolution not to consent to any sin, however small, is a sure sign that we are in God's grace."2 But

1 *Life*, ch. 11.
2 *Spirit of St Francis de Sales*, ch. 4.

[466] a soul in profound desolation cannot even clearly discern this resolution; nevertheless, in such a state she must not aim at feeling what she wills; it is enough to will with the point of the will. In this manner she should

entirely abandon herself into the arms of the divine goodness. Oh, how do such acts of confidence and resignation
ravish the heart of God, when made in the midst of the
darkness of desolation! Ah, let us simply trust in a God,
who (as St. Teresa says) loves us far better than we love
ourselves.

Let these souls, then, so dear to God, and who are resolutely determined to belong entirely to him, take comfort, although at the same time they see themselves
deprived of every consolation. Their desolation is a
sign of their being very acceptable to God, and that he
has for them a place prepared in his heavenly kingdom,
which overflows with consolations as full as they are
lasting. And let them hold for certain, that the more
they are afflicted in the present life, so much the more
they shall be consoled in eternity: *According to the multi-
tude of my sorrows in my heart, Your comforts have given
joy to my soul.*1

Example

For the encouragement of souls in desolation, I will
here mention what is related in the life of St. Jane
Frances de Chantal.

For the space of forty years she was tormented by the
most fearful interior trials, by temptations, by fears of
being in enmity with God, and of being even quite forsaken by him. Her afflictions were so excruciating and
unremitting, that she declared her sole ray of comfort
came from the thought of death. Moreover she said:
"I am so furiously assaulted, that I know not where to

1 "Secundum multitudinem dolorum meorum in corde meo, con-

solationes tunc laetificaverunt animam meam." Ps. 93.19.

[467] hide my poor soul. I seem at times on the point of losing all patience, and of giving up all as utterly lost." "The tyrant of temptation is so relentless," she says, "that any hour of the day I would gladly barter it with the loss of my life; and sometimes it happens that I can neither eat nor sleep."1

During the last eight or nine years of her life, her temptations became still more violent. Mother de Chatel said that her saintly Mother de Chantal suffered a continual interior martyrdom night and day, at prayer, at work, and even during sleep; so that she felt the deepest compassion for her. The saint endured assaults against every virtue (except chastity), and had likewise to contend with doubts, darkness, and disgust. Sometimes God would withdraw all lights from her, and seem indignant with her, and just on the point of expelling her from him; so that terror drove her to look in some other direction for relief: but failing to find any, she was obliged to return to look on God, and to abandon herself to his mercy. She seemed each moment ready to yield to the violence of her temptations. The divine assistance did not indeed forsake her; but it seemed to her to have done so, since, instead of finding satisfaction in anything, she found only weariness and anguish in prayer, in reading spiritual books, in Communion, and in all other exercises of piety. Her sole resource in this state of dereliction was to look upon God, and to let him do his will.

The saint said: "In all my abandonments my mere life is a new cross to me, and my incapability of action adds considerably to its heaviness." And it was there-

fore that she compared herself to a sick person over
whelmed with sufferings, unable to turn from one side to
the other, speechless, so as not to be able to express his

1 *Mem. de la M. de Chaugy*, Pt. 3, ch. 27.

[468] ills, and blind, so as not to discern whether the attend-
ants are administering to him medicine or poison. And
then, weeping bitterly, she added, "I seem to be without
faith, without hope, and without love for my God."
Nevertheless, the saint maintained throughout her serenity of countenance and affability in conversation, and
kept her looks fixedly bent towards God, in the bosom
of whose blessed will she constantly reposed. And so
St. Francis de Sales, who was her director, and knew
well what an object of predilection her beautiful soul
was to Almighty God, wrote thus of her: "Her heart
resembled a deaf musician, who, though he may sing
most exquisitely, can derive no pleasure from it himself."
And to herself he wrote as follows: "You must endeavor
to serve your Savior solely through love of his blessed
will, utterly deprived of consolations, and overwhelmed
by a deluge of fears and sadness."1 It is thus that the
saints are formed:

"Long did the chisels ring around,
Long did the mallet's blows rebound,
Long worked the head and toiled the hand,
Ere stood your stones as now they stand."2

The saints of whom the Church sings are precisely these
choice stones, which are reduced to shapeliness and
beauty by the strokes of the chisel, that is, by temptations, by fears, by darkness, and other torments, internal
and external, till at length they are made worthy to be

enthroned in the blessed kingdom of Paradise.

1 *Love of God,* Bk. 9, ch. 11.
2 "Scalpri salubris ictibus
Et tunsione plurima,
Fabri polita malleo,
Hanc saxa molem construunt,
Aptisque juncta nexibus
Locantur in fastigio." *Offic. Dedic. eccl.*

Affections and Prayers

[469] O Jesus, my hope, my love and only love of my soul,
I deserve not Your consolations and sweet visitations; keep
them for those innocent souls that have always loved You;
sinner that I am, I do not deserve them, nor do I ask for them:
this only do I ask, give me grace to love You, to accomplish
Your adorable will during my whole life; and then dispose of
me as You please! Unhappy me! far other darkness, other ter-
rors, other abandonments would be due to the outrages which
I have done You: hell were my just award, where, separated
from You forever, and totally abandoned by You, I should shed
tears eternally, without ever being able to love You more. But
no, my Jesus, I accept of every punishment; only spare me this.
You are deserving of an infinite love; You have placed me under
an excessive obligation of loving You; oh, no, I cannot trust
my self to live and not love You! I do love You, my sovereign
good; I love You with my whole heart; I love You more
than myself; I love You, and have no other desire than to love
You. I own that this my good-will is the pure effect of Your
grace; but do You, O my Lord, perfect Your own work; with
draw not Your helping hand till death! Oh, never for a moment
leave me in my own hands; give me strength to vanquish
temptations and to overcome myself; and for this end give me
grace always to have recourse to You! I wish to belong

wholly to You; I give You my body, my soul, my will, and my liberty; I will no longer live for myself, but for You alone, my Creator, my Redeemer, my love, and my all: my God and my all. 1 I desire to become a saint, and I hope this of You. Afflict me as You will, deprive me of all; only deprive me not of Your grace and of Your love.

O Mary, the hope of sinners, great is your power with God; I confide fully in your intercession: I entreat you by your love of Jesus Christ, help me, and make me a saint!

1 "Deus meus et omnia."

Summary of the Virtues Necessary for Those Who Seek to Love Jesus Christ

I.

[470] We must patiently endure the trials of this life - ill health, sorrows, poverty, losses, loss of loved ones, insults, persecutions, and all that is disagreeable. Let us invariably look on the sufferings of this life as signs of God's love towards us, and of his desire to save us in the world to come. And let us, moreover, be fully persuaded that the involuntary mortifications which God himself sends us are far more pleasing to him than those which are the result of our own choosing.

In sickness let us endeavor to resign ourselves entirely to the will of God; no devout exercise is more acceptable to him than this. If at such times we are unable to meditate, let us fix our eyes on our crucified Lord, and offer him our sufferings in union with all that he endured for us upon the cross. And when we are told that we are about to die, let us accept the news with tranquility and in the spirit of sacrifice; that is, with the desire to die, in order to give pleasure to Jesus Christ: it was this desire that gave great merit to the death of the martyrs. We should then say: O Lord, behold me here with no other will but Your own blessed will; I am willing to suffer as much as You please; I wish to die whenever You will. Nor should we then wish to have our life prolonged, in order to do penance for our sins; to accept death with perfect resignation outweighs all other penance.

We must likewise practice conformity to the will of God in bearing poverty and the various inconveniences [471] which accompany it: cold, hunger, fatigue, contempt, and scorn.

Nor should we be less resigned to losses, whether of property or of relatives and friends, on whom our comfort and happiness depended. Let us acquire the good habit of saying in every adversity: God has so willed it, and so I will it likewise. And at the death of our relatives, instead of wasting time in fruitless excessive grieving, let us employ it in praying for their souls; and offer to Jesus Christ, in their behalf, the pain of our bereavement.

Let us, moreover, force ourselves to endure scorn and insult with patience and tranquility. Let us answer terms of insult and injury with words of gentleness; but as long as we feel ourselves disturbed, the best plan is to keep silence, till the mind grows tranquil. Meanwhile let us not be fretfully speaking to others of the offense we have received, but in silence offer it to Jesus Christ, who endured so much for us.

II.

Behave kindly to all, to those in authority and inferiors, to the high-born and low-born, to relatives and strangers; but more especially to the poor and to the sick, and above all to those who dislike us.

Gentleness in the correction of others' faults is more efficacious than any other means that may be employed. Be therefore on your guard against correcting in a fit of passion; for then harshness is sure to be mingled with it, either in word or action. Beware likewise of correcting the person at fault while he is excited; for in like cases the result is exasperation instead of improvement.

III.

Envy not the great ones of this world their riches, honors, dignities, or applause given them by men; but [472] envy rather those who most love Jesus Christ, who undoubtedly enjoy greater happiness than the great ones of this world. Return thanks to the Lord for enlightening you to discover the vanity of all worldly things, for the sake of which so many unhappily perish.

IV.

In all our actions and thoughts let us seek only the pleasure of Almighty God, and not our private satisfaction; and let us therefore lay aside all disappointment when our efforts seem to fail. And when we succeed, let us be no less cautious against seeking the thanks and approval of others; should they murmur against us, let us pay no attention to this; our consola-

tion will be to have striven to please God, and not
men.

V.

The chief means of perfection are:

1. To avoid all deliberate sin, however small. Should
we, however, happen unfortunately to commit a fault,
let us refrain from becoming angry and impatient with
ourselves: we must, on such occasions, quietly repent of
it; and while we make an act of love to Jesus Christ,
and beg his help, we must promise him not to repeat the
fault.

2. To have an earnest desire to acquire the perfection
of the saints, and to suffer all things to please Jesus
Christ; and if we have not this desire, to beseech Jesus
Christ, through his goodness, to grant it to us; since, as long
as we do not feel a sincere desire of becoming saints, we
shall never make one step forward in the way of perfection.

3. To have a firm resolution of arriving at perfection:
whoever is lacking in this resolution, works but half-
heartedly, and will not overcome their natural defects;
[473] whereas a resolute soul, with the unfailing help of
God, overcomes every obstacle.

4. To make daily two hours or at least one hour
[Scripture and other spiritual reading with] of mental
prayer; and, except in case of urgent necessity,
never to relinquish it for the sake of any weariness,
dryness, or trouble that we may experience.

5. To frequent Holy Communion several times a week....
With regard to external mortifications, such as fasting, etc.,
they should be practiced in obedience to our spiritual
director, otherwise they will either destroy health or
produce vainglory. So that it is necessary for each one to
have his own director, so that all maybe regulated in obedience to him.

6. To pray continually, by having recourse to Jesus
Christ in all our necessities, by invoking likewise the intercession of our Angel Guardian, of our Holy Patrons,
and most particularly of the Blessed Mother, through
whose hands Almighty God bestows all graces upon us.
It has already been shown, at the end of Chapter 4, that
our welfare entirely depends on prayer. We must especially not pass a day without begging God to grant us
the gift of perseverance in his grace; whoever asks
for this perseverance obtains it, but he that does not
ask for it obtains it not, and is damned: we must pray,
too, that Jesus Christ may grant us his holy love and perfect conformity with his divine will. Neither should we
forget to pray for every grace through the merits of Jesus
Christ. We must first offer these prayers when we rise
in the morning, and afterwards repeat them in our meditation, at Holy Communion, at the visit to the Blessed
Sacrament, and again in the evening at the examination
of conscience. We must particularly cry to God for help
[474] in the time of temptation, and more especially in
temptations against purity, when we should not cease to
call for help on the holy names of Jesus and Mary. He
that prays, conquers; he that prays not, is conquered.

VI.

With respect to humility, not to pride ourselves on

riches, honors, high birth, talents, or any other natural advantage, and still less on any spiritual gift, realizing that all are the gifts of God. To consider ourselves the worst of all, and consequently to delight in being despised by others; and not to act as some do, who declare themselves the worst of men, and at the same time wish to be treated as the best. Moreover, to receive corrections humbly, and without attempts to excuse ourselves, and this even though blamed wrongfully; except when to defend ourselves would be necessary in order to prevent others being scandalized.

Much more ought we to banish all desire of appearing in public, and of being honored by the world. The maxim of St. Francis should never be out of our sight: "We are just what we are before God." It would be still worse for a religious to covet posts of honor and superiority in his community. The true honor of a religious is to be the most humble of all; and he is the humblest of all who most joyfully embraces humiliations.

VII.

Detach your heart from all creatures. Whoever continues bound by the slightest fondness to things of earth can never rise to a perfect union with God.

To detach ourselves especially from an undue affection for our relatives. It was said by St. Philip Neri, that "whatever affection we bestow on creatures is so much [475] taken from God."1 In deciding on a state of life, we must be quite unbiased by the advice of parents, who generally keep their own interests in view, rather than our real welfare.

Cast away all considerations of human respect, and of the vain esteem of men; and, above all, be detached from self-will. We must leave all, in order to gain all. "All for all,"2 writes Thomas a Kempis.

VIII.

Not to give way to anger, whatever happens; but if by chance the sparks of passion are suddenly lighted in our breasts, let us call on God, and refrain from acting or speaking till we are sure that our anger is appeased. We shall find it of great service to arm ourselves in prayer against every chance of irritation that may befall us, in order not then to give way to culpable resentment; we should always remember that saying of St. Francis de Sales: "I never remember to have been angry with out afterwards regretting it."

IX.

All sanctity consists in loving God, and all love of God consists in doing his blessed will. We must, therefore, bow with resignation to all the dispositions of divine Providence without reserve; and so cheerfully submit to the adversity as well as prosperity which God sends, to the state of life in which God places us, to the sort of health which God bestows on us: and this should be the primary aim of all our prayers, namely, that God would enable us to fulfill his holy will in all things. And in order to be certain of the divine will, the religious must depend on obedience to his Superior, and those who are in the world to their confessor; for nothing is more cer-

1 *Bacci*, Bk. 2, ch. 15.

2 "Totum pro toto." *Imitation of Christ*, Bk. 3, ch. 37.

[476] tain than that saying of St. Philip Neri: "We shall
have no account to render to God of what is done through
obedience." Which is to be understood, of course, as
long as there is no evident sin in the command.

X.

There are two remedies against temptations: resignation and prayer. Resignation, for though temptations do
not come from God, yet he permits them for our good.
So beware of yielding to discouragement, however an-
noying the temptations may be; be resigned to the will
of God, who allows them; and take up the arms of
prayer, which are the most powerful and the most certain to overcome our enemies. Bad thoughts, however
filthy and ugly, are not sins; it is only the consenting
to them which makes the sin. We shall never be overcome as long as we call on the holy names of Jesus
and Mary. During the assaults of temptation, it is of
help to renew our resolution to suffer death rather
than to offend God; it is also a good practice repeatedly to sign ourselves with the sign of the cross, and
with holy water; it is of great help, too, to reveal the
temptation to our confessor. But prayer is the most
necessary remedy, and continual cries for help to Jesus
and Mary.

XI.

Then as to spiritual desolations, there are two acts in
which we ought principally to exercise ourselves: 1st, to
humble ourselves, with the sincere acknowledgment that we
deserve no better treatment; 2nd, to resign ourselves to the

will of God, and to abandon ourselves into the arms of his divine goodness. When God favors us with consolations, let us prepare ourselves for coming trials, which generally follow consolations. If it please God to leave us in desolation, let us be humble and fully resigned to [477] his divine will, and we shall thus reap far greater advantage from desolations than from consolations.

XII.

In order to live always well, we must store up deeply in our minds certain general maxims of eternal life, such as the following:

1. All passes away in this life, whether it be joy or sorrow; but in eternity nothing passes away.
2. What good is all the greatness of this world at the hour of death?
3. All that comes from God, whether it be adverse or prosperous, all is good, and is for our welfare.
4. We must leave all, to gain all.
5. There is no peace to be found without God.
6. To love God and save one's soul is the one thing necessary.
7. We need only be afraid of sin.
8. If God be lost, all is lost.
9. He that desires nothing in this world is master of the whole world.
10. He that prays is saved, and he that does not pray is damned.
11. Let me die, if it gives God pleasure.
12. God is cheap at any cost.
13. Every pain is light to him who has deserved hell.
14. He is able to endure all who looks on Jesus crucified.
15. Everything turns into pain that is not done for God.

16. Whoever wishes for God alone is rich in every good.
17. Happy the man who can say: "My Jesus, I desire
You alone, and nothing more!"
18. He who loves God, finds pleasure in everything; he
who does not love God, finds no true pleasure in anything.

[478] HYMNS ON THE SACRED HEART OF JESUS.*

1. The Loving Spouse

FLY, my soul, ah, fly away
To Jesus heart so kind;
There love's captive you shall stay,
And truest freedom find.

See, your foes are all around;
You are pursued, poor thing!
Safety in the ark is found,
To there, O dove, take wing.

Why delay? The world is woe,
And care, and cold deceit;
God alone can joy bestow,
And happiness complete.

Give me, Lord, a place to dwell
Within Your heart so meek;
This shall be my prison cell,
Where true repose I seek.

All on earth I now disdain,
And for Your love resign;
This the fruit of every pain,
To bind my heart to Your.

If within Your heart divine
To die my lot should be,
Oh, what happy death were mine!
Such death were life to me.

* St. Alphonsus, in adopting these two hymns and inserting them among his works, informs us that they were composed by another author, whom he does not name. ED.

2. The Loving Spouse in the Heart of Jesus

I DWELL a captive in this heart,
On fire with love divine;
'Tis here I live alone in peace,
And constant joy is mine.

It is the Heart of God's own Son,
In his humanity,
Who, all enamored of my soul,
Here burns with love of me.

Here, like the dove within the ark,
Securely I repose;
Since now the Lord is my defense,
I fear no earthly foes.

Now I have found this happy home,
God's love alone I prize;
All else is torment to my heart,
The world I now despise.

What though I suffer, still in love
I ever true will be;

My love of God shall deeper grow
When crosses fall on me.

Then he who longs with me to seek
Repose within this nest,
All love that is not love for God,
Must banish from his breast.

You haughty lovers of the world,
Full of self-love, depart!
Away, away! no place is found
For you within this heart.

Each vile and earthly chain impedes
The soul's true heavenward flight;
All, all the heart belongs to God,
Love claims his sovereign right.

From every bond of earth, dear Lord,
Your grace has set me free;
My soul, delivered from the snare,
Enjoys true liberty.

I cannot love You as I ought,
This pains me, this alone;
For all my love must have an end;
Your goodness, Lord, has none.

One thought brings comfort to my heart-
I love a good so great,
That though I love him all I can,
More love he merits yet.

Naught more can I desire than this,
To see his face in heav'n;

And this I hope, since he on earth
His heart in pledge has given.

Supplement: A poem by Darrell Wright

Love is...

Love is patient, love is kind;
All selfish ways it leaves behind.
Love is never harsh or rude;
It governs every changing mood.
Love is generous in giving,
Bears all things and is forgiving.
Love is trusting, never jealous;
For God and neighbor it is zealous.
Love that's true will never fail;
It's always new, it's never stale.
Love dispels all hateful wrath;
It takes the peaceful, gentle path.
Love will never put on airs;
With joy it serves; it always cares.
With love one never seeks oneself:
In giving, it draws down God's wealth.
Love that's true is always pure:
Thus blessed by God, it shall endure.
Love is strong and persevering,
Ever faithful, never fearing.
Love is patient, love is kind;
With love, God's kingdom you shall find.
(Cf. 1 Cor. 13:4-8)

INDEX

divine
will, 321 ; his patience in sickness, 416; how he triumphed over
the two passions, anger and love, 395.
FRIENDSHIP, it presupposes a communication of goods, 437.
GOD, his love for us, his benefits, 264; he loves to see us suffer, but
this is for our good, 428.
HENRY Suso, Blessed, learns by revelation the trials that await him,
426.
HOLY SPIRIT, our divine love, novena, 478; effects that he
produces in souls, meditations, 479; pious exercise to obtain his
gifts, 496; hymn, 505.
HOPE, it augments charity, 434.
HUMILITY, its necessity and its merit, 358; the practice of it, 361;
we must avoid vainglory, 366.
INTENTION, pure, to please God, necessary in all our actions, 323;
which are signs of it, 326.
JANE Frances de Chantal, St., her interior trials, 466.
JESUS CHRIST, love that he has shown us by suffering for us, 265;
by instituting the Blessed Sacrament, 275; desire that he has to be
united to us, 279; confidence with which this love of our Savior
should inspire us, 285; how much we are obliged to love him, 293;
how we should love him, 299; he wishes to be loved alone without a
competitor, 372.
JOHN of the Cross, St., chooses a house in which he has more to
suffer, 427.
JONAS, St., Martyr, his resignation sustained by the remembrance
of Jesus crucified, 418.
JOSEPH, St., de Leonissa, his courage in a painful operation, 418.
LIDWINE, St., her resignation in sufferings, 418; thereby she
completed her crown, 419.
LOVE, divine, its excellence, 297; its marks, 300; the practice of it,
305; it perfects faith, 430; and makes hope increase, 435. See Holy
Ghost and Perfection.
LUKEWARMNESS, unavoidable, 330; lukewarmness that one can
and should avoid, 331; remedies against this vice, 334, 472, 477.
MARGARET of the Cross, Sister, prefers a poor habit to the purple,
MEEKNESS, its excellence, the practice of it, 316, 392, 471, 475.
MORTIFICATIONS, those that come from God or from our
neighbor are preferable to those of our own choice, 313; exterior
mortifications are necessary, 460. Interior mortification, see

Detachment.

OBEDIENCE, sure means to fulfill God's will, 409; it should subject the will and the judgment, 412. Seculars practice obedience by submitting to their confessor, 412.

ORDERS, holy, sanctity required for receiving them, 382.

PARADISE, we should desire it in order to love God perfectly; in this consists the happiness of the soul, 440.

PATIENCE, its necessity and its merit, 305; it renders us happy even in this life, 310. Patience in sickness, 415; in poverty, 421; in the loss of relatives and friends, 425; in contempt, 426. Practical summary, 470.

PERFECTION, it consists solely in the love of God, 263, 299; or in humility, mortification, and conformity to the divine will, 406; means to attain it and persevering in it, 272, 334, 472, 494.

PETER, Martyr, St., Jesus crucified appears to him in prison, 427.

PHILIP Neri, St., prefers the house in which he has more to suffer, 426.

POVERTY, we should patiently bear it and even love it, 421.

PRAYER, its necessity and efficacy, 351; especially against temptations, 450, 476.

The Lord's prayer, explanation, 48. Mental prayer, its utility and importance, 342; subjects for meditation, 346.

PURGATORY, the greatest pain that one suffers there, and particular pain for those that have but little desire for heaven, 445.

SICKNESS, with what patience one should bear it, 415.

SOUL, its happiness and its union with God in heaven, 442.

SUFFERINGS, their utility, 305. See Patience.

SUPERIOR, what should be his meekness, 317.

TEMPTATIONS, pains that they cause a soul that loves Jesus Christ, and why God permits them, 447; means to be adopted to conquer them, 450, 476.

TERESA, St., Jesus encourages her to suffer, 418.

VINCENT de Paul, St., his meekness, 320; his patience in sickness, 415, 417.

VOCATION, one is not obliged to obey one's parents when there is question of following it, 381; signs of vocation to the ecclesiastical state, 382.